# From Grief to Glory

## A Personal Journey From Darkness Into Light

*Francine Lolacono-Bouwense*

From Grief to Glory
by Francine Lolacono-Bouwense

Printed in the United States of America
ISBN 1-931232-32-6

Unless otherwise indicated, Bible quotations are taken from The New International Version, Copyright 1973, 1978, 1984 by International Bible Society.

Xulon Press
344 Maple Ave. West, #302
Vienna, VA 22180
703-691-7595
XulonPress.com

"Consider it pure joy, my brothers,
whenever you face trials of many kinds,
because you know that the testing
of your faith develops perseverance.
Perseverance must finish its work
so that you may be mature and complete,
not lacking anything."

(James 1: 2 - 4)

# Dedication

I dedicate this book to the memory of my dear sister and brother, Jeanne K. Lo Iacono and Vincent S. Lo Iacono, Jr. As twins, they entered the world at nearly the same time. Thirty-six years later, they entered into what I believe is eternal glory, at nearly the same time.

# Contents

# Acknowledgements

I need to thank many people, because I did not complete this work alone. Many thanks to:

- Spyro S. Matthews—for spending hour upon hour, self-lessly sharing your talents to make this work what it is. You took the manuscript and helped me turn it into a book. You are a gift from God.

- Reverend John Franco—for your technical expertise, time, and support.

- My husband, Randy—your strong arms held me up when I was down. Your reassuring words grounded me when I almost lost my way. You inspired me to write this book. I love you!

- My parents, Vincent and Frances—you bravely endured the pain of losing two children and still "kept the faith."

- Extended family and friends—your love and support was a blessing during a very dark time.

# Preface

I wrote this book with two purposes in mind. First, the book is intended to provide comfort and healing for those who find themselves in a place of despair, as a result of losing a "significant person" in their life. It is for individuals who have abandoned the hope of having a meaningful and happy future because of their loss.

While "loss," referred to in this book, focuses on the end of a human life, loss cannot and should not be limited to that meaning alone. Loss can be the end of a relationship or the end of a particular "season" of your life. It can be anything that you have to say "good-bye" to and are having difficulty letting go of. If you have experienced other kinds of loss in your life, I believe you too can draw much from this writing.

Second, the book was written for those of us who attempt to learn from life's experiences. It was written for those of us who seek to draw a deeper understanding of "life's lessons" through both the struggles and pleasures this life can bring. It is for the person interested in personal, spiritual growth.

This is an account of my personal journey from grief to glory. Though it is *my* account, I have not made this journey alone. Both the grief and the journey involve my family, as this grief stemmed from the loss of two of our family members. While we have each had to individually face and deal with our own personal issues relating to this grief, we have tried to help each other and experience this journey together, where we could. I shall briefly acquaint you with my family, as I refer to them frequently throughout the book.

My parents first met in the late 1950's in Lodi, New Jersey. My mom, a Polish-American, was working in an Italian pastry shop during her high school years. My dad, an Italian-American, used to pick up the baked goods for his family on Sundays at this same pastry shop. After he saw my mother working behind the counter, he began bringing home cakes, rolls and cannolis on weekdays too! My grandmother thought my father was such a good son, always thinking of his parents and brothers. She soon came to realize that my dad was frequenting the pastry shop as a way of seeing my mother. My parents were married in 1959.

The newlyweds had little time alone as a couple, as they were endowed with children soon after they were married. Nancy was the first—born ten months following their wedding. Eleven months later, my mother gave birth to twins. Jeanne and Vinnie Jr. were born two and a half months premature. They were very sick, but through the grace of God, they survived. Two years later I was born and two years after that my brother Stephen was born. When you do the math, that is five children in five years. My parents struggled, but with God's help, they made it and lived to tell the tale.

We were an average middle-class family of seven, living in the suburbs of New Jersey. My dad worked hard to support his wife and five children in his family-owned casket manufacturing business, begun by my grandfather in the 1940's. My mom worked equally hard raising her family and working with my father in the casket business. My brothers and sisters and I were all raised with a strong work ethic. My dad took one or two of us to work with him every Saturday, usually to clean the building or finish up the filing in the office that didn't get done during the week. It doesn't sound like much on paper, but it was a really big deal to us kids and provided some early and valuable lessons in responsibility.

My folks took us to church every Sunday, taught us the difference between right and wrong, and raised us to be good, decent people. In particular, I remember my parents both modeling and preaching the concept of "doing the right thing" till they were blue in the face. In today's vernacular, that translates into "living a life of integrity."

Over the years, we shared many happy times, as well as sad. We children kept our parents very busy by participating in sporting events, school clubs and committees, choral presentations, church activities and the like. We took vacations together down the Jersey shore in the reliable wood-paneled station wagon. We had many family parties for birthdays, communions, anniversaries, graduations, and weddings. Our house was full of fun and fighting, celebration and chaos. I believe we gave our parents much joy and pleasure, but plenty of aggravation and gray hair as well.

Although we all lived under the same roof with generally the same set of rules and values, my siblings and I grew up very different from each other. We were each blessed with different gifts, personalities, and temperaments. Some of us excelled in academics, some in sports, some had musical abilities, while some had a gift for connecting with people. My brothers and sisters and I each pursued very different career paths. Nancy pursued a career in medical research, while Jeanne chose a career in education. Vinnie started out as an industrial engineer and eventually became a self-employed landscaper. I became a physical therapist, and my brother Stephen followed in my dad's footsteps, working in the family business.

All in all, my family seemed like an ordinary American family, and we were. But as you will see, sometimes extraordinary things happen to ordinary people that forever change their lives.

The idea for this book was birthed as a direct result of the deaths of my sister Jeanne and my brother Vinnie. My sister died on April 28, 1997 from breast cancer. After watching her battle the disease for a year and a half and then finally die, I thought things were about as bad as they could get. I was sorely mistaken. Just four and a half months later, on September 12, 1997, my brother Vinnie was found dead after suffering a heart attack in his sleep. My sister and brother were both 36 years young. These two tragic events have brought forth some poignant, unexpected lessons pertaining to living life well and to finding the strength and courage to go on living, even when living is painful.

Through my journey of grief, I have looked back on my sister's and brother's lives and the events surrounding their deaths. I have contemplated my role and influence in both their lives and deaths, as well as the role and influence of others. As a result of much reflection, many simple yet significant lessons have literally jumped out at me. It is not the first time that I have considered these principles that I call lessons in this book. Rather, the experience of losing my siblings has made these principles come alive for me in a way that they never had before. Additionally, I have learned to tap into the only true and lasting source of comfort, peace, and healing for my broken heart. When the world could not bring me solace, the love of God and His Word could.

I do not believe that I have learned all there is to learn. Nevertheless, I have thus far drawn much from these experiences. At this juncture in my life, I am compelled to put what I have learned on paper, for others to read. My very tears have been poured out onto the pages of this book. But as they fell and as I continued to write, a catharsis took place. Those tears of sorrow and mourning were turned into joy, gladness, and Godly insight.

I allow myself to be purposely transparent because if you are to appreciate where God has brought me, you must see the truth of where I was and how I got there. You must also see how I got to be where I am *today*. Thus, it is my hope to convey to you these lessons that I have learned, for the purpose of exhorting and edifying you and to offer you peace, comfort, hope, joy, and guidance, wherever you are in your life today. I believe they are lessons straight from the heart of God. By no means have I fully assimilated these lessons into my life yet, but I am working toward that goal, with His grace.

As you read, you will notice that each chapter has a theme or basic lesson to be relayed. Underlining the lesson are scriptures for the purpose of securing the theme. It is my belief that all answers to life's problems are found in the Word of God, the Holy Bible. I believe that the Bible is the inspired Word of God, and I always look to God's Word for wisdom and clarity. I include my personal experiences and the lessons learned from those experiences, but I use the Holy Scriptures as the anchoring source for my thoughts in this book because this is how I live my life. It is the best way I know how to live. In and of myself, I have nothing to write which is worthy of reading. It is God's thoughts and words that are worthy and that which I wish to come through on these pages.

I believe it is important to mention that, technically, there is a difference between the meanings of the words "grieve" and "mourn." Depending on where in the Bible these words are used, they take on different connotations. For simplicity's sake, I use the words "grieve or grief" and "mourn or mourning" interchangeably. That is, throughout this book, the words grief and mourning are to mean simply, "experiencing, processing, expressing or coping with the pain that follows significant loss." This is in stark contrast to the idea of a "spirit of grief." A "spirit of grief," by definition, is a heavy weight or oppressive burden. Indeed, you will see that I did battle with this oppression. But my synonymous use of "grieve and mourn" is in no way intended to encourage the reader to entertain a spirit of grief. In fact, quite the opposite. I trust the substance of this text will bear this out.

I pray that the experiences shared in this "labor of love" will bring you comfort, inspiration, hope, and wisdom. May they not be just "nice words" to read, but may these truths become the substance that can feed the hungry and hurt soul that has been neglected thus far. May they become realities in your life.

# Chapter One

# Joy Comes In the Morning

I begin with this chapter so that anyone reading this book who has suffered great loss can know that they too can live and be happy again. I write this with deep conviction, as I have endured great loss yet am beginning to do just that: both live and be happy again. You may be thinking that my loss and others' losses are not as great as yours. You may feel that there is something unique and more profound to your grief than that of everyone else's which precludes you from ever finding happiness or even having a reason to live again.

Certainly every situation carries with it special circumstances and thus its own unique pain. Admittedly, some situations are more difficult to bear than others. In fact they may seem absolutely unbearable. Even so, at the risk of sounding trite, I tell you the truth: God has *whatever* you need. Whether you lost a child, a spouse, a parent, a sibling, a close relative, or a beloved friend, the truth is the same. Whether your loss came by way of sickness, accident, homicide, suicide, or some other way, the truth remains unchanged. *"The truth,"* is what God says in His

Word about your situation, and assuredly I tell you, "the truth
will set you free" (John 8: 32).

---

**I wish to show you that God has the
ability and desire to raise you up to
new heights with Him, no matter
where you find yourself today.**

---

I wish to show you that *God has the ability and desire to raise you up
to new heights with Him*, no matter where you find yourself today.
God did this very thing for me. But before I show you the
heights He has taken me *to*, I need to show you the depths He
has taken me *out of*.

I understand the gut-wrenching pain that can fill your belly.
The kind of pain that is so tormenting, it prevents you from
sleeping at night; but when it is morning, you don't know how
you will get out of bed. The anguish can be so far-reaching into
the inner most core of your being, you can hardly imagine such
a depth of pain could exist.

You see, my family and I watched my sister Jeanne battle
breast cancer for a year and a half. We were with her through the
painful surgeries, the chemotherapy and radiation treatments,
and all of the nasty experiences that usually attach themselves
to such a condition.

In particular, I had the horrifying encounter of watching
Jeanne experience what would be the first of many seizures
during her last days of suffering in the hospital. My mother and
I were merely trying to situate her head on the pillow to make
her more comfortable when the seizure began. Terrified, my
mother and I were rushed out of the room while the hospital

staff attended to her. No one understood at that moment what was happening. My father and husband, in the hallway, demanded, "What's happening?" We thought that she was going into cardiac arrest and that this was the end. My parents began crying and shaking, and I yelled to my husband to grab them. Fear began to grip me as I began a low sob and a call to Jesus in a high-pitched squeal. My father yelled to my husband, "Get Francine!" You see, I was seven months pregnant. I am certain I will never forget the scene.

After several days of this kind of horror, my parents prayed that God would take their very sick daughter out of her misery. A prayer like that can only be propelled out of a sacrificial love. At her funeral, I watched my father angst, "Why *her* Lord, why not *me*?" because only nine months prior to Jeanne getting sick, my father was diagnosed with thyroid cancer.

After going through what felt like a two-and-a-half- year hellish nightmare, there seemed to be better days ahead. My father was recovering from the bout of cancer he had faced. It was May of 1997, and I had just completed five years of graduate school for an MBA at Fairleigh Dickinson University. At eight months pregnant, I remember feeling like I was wearing a tent rather than a graduation gown. As I took my assigned seat, I remember feeling sad that Jeanne could not be at my graduation. But I looked up to heaven during the ceremony, thinking of her, and I knew that she would have been proud of me. We had our new baby to look forward to, and my husband, daughter, and I were also moving to a new home in the country. In July, our beautiful baby boy was born, and three weeks later we moved. So much had happened in such a short time, that needless to say, I was exhausted.

It was now September, and my husband and I decided to go on vacation. We needed to recuperate from all that had gone on. Our plan was to get as much rest as any couple can, given that we had our three and a half-year-old daughter and two-month-old baby boy with us.

The majority of the week had passed rather uneventfully. That would soon change. On Thursday night of our vacation week, I felt a strong unction in my spirit to pray, especially for my brother Vinnie. I began praying at about 11:00 p.m., mostly for my brother. I was burdened for him, as I knew that he was having an especially difficult time grieving for his twin sister. I finished at about 1 a.m. and, reluctantly, went to bed.

The next morning, my husband woke me and paced the room in a circle. He look nauseated and kept saying, "Oh honey, oh God! You have to stay calm. Remember, the kids are here." After what seemed to be an hour, but in reality was probably one minute, I yelled, "What happened! Please... tell me!" He sat beside me on the bed and squarely faced me. And then his words slammed into my face like a brick wall: "Your mother just called... your brother Vinnie died." At first I had no reaction. I responded to my husband's news with a blank stare. Seconds later, the reality of my husband's words registered in my brain. I dug my fingers into his arms, my face pressed into his chest, my body rocking back and forth, as I let go guttural sobs, "No... it can't be... not my Vinnie! Vinnie! Vinnie! VINNIE!"

Shortly after receiving the news, we ended our vacation and began the five hour trek to my parents' house in near silence. I stared out the car window as if in a trance. The only words my husband and I exchanged were tearful questions about what could have possibly happened to my brother. We could not make sense of it.

We arrived at my parents' home late Friday night. I could tell by all of the cars parked out front that many of our relatives had already gathered at the house. We were the furthest away and, consequently, the last to arrive. Even though I was eager to see my family since hearing the news in the morning, I found myself dreading the idea of walking into the house. What happened next is indelibly engraved in my mind.

I walked in the back door. Though many people were in the house, there was a loud silence present. The air was heavy with grief and oppression. As I walked down the short corridor to the kitchen, I spied my mother's face contorted with pain. My aunts and uncles fearfully anticipated the next outburst of emotional agony. I hugged my mother as we cried, unable to speak. Next, I embraced my father. We sobbed in each other's arms as I yelled, "Why Dad, why? What's going on?" He only moaned back, "I don't understand Fran. I don't know what's going on." My mother looked away and screamed, "All we do is cry in this house. It's not fair, it's just not fair!" Finally, my sister and I grabbed each other, crying. We said very little, but the intensity of the grip that we had on each other said a lot. We held on tightly, each of us fearing the other to be next. We were afraid to let go. I entered the kitchen trembling, observing family members either crying or silently shaking their downcast heads in disbelief. In that moment, I had wondered if this was a sneak preview of what hell was like.

There are two sayings that well-meaning people tried to remind me of after the passing of my brother and sister: "Take one day at a time" and "Time heals all wounds." I remember wondering, in response to these clichés, how I would get through the next hour and sometimes minutes because the despair was so great, never mind the day. And my most vivid imaginations could not fathom ever being healed of this painful trauma. But of this I am sure: *joy comes in the morning.*

Even in those horribly dark moments at my parents' house, just hours after my brother died, God had already begun His work, sowing seeds of healing and hope. After things quieted down a bit, I remember hearing a soft, sweet little sound. Everyone sitting around the kitchen table had heard it too. We stopped to see what it was. It was our little baby, Christian, cooing and gurgling and smiling. Amidst the anguish, we just stared and listened, happy to experience a small break in the pain. Little by little, our faces brightened. I was amazed and grateful at how God could infuse light, though it seemed like only a small glimmer at the time, into a very dark situation.

I will never wonder about the timing of my son's birth. It was divinely planned. Not that anyone could ever take another's place, but when Jeanne was taken from our family, it helped me to look forward to the promise of new life yet to come in our unborn baby. And when Vinnie died, I clung to my infant, desperate for solace. As I nursed him, though he was drawing nourishment from me, I was drawing comfort and strength from him in those early days.

That night, September 12th, 1997, in my parents' kitchen, I saw God's hand at work through a very simple everyday occurrence of a baby's cooing. It was the first ray of hope, visible to me, for my family's future, after these tragedies. One of the early Christian writers said, "A ray of God's light can bring healing to a lot of dark places." Look for that ray of hope in your situation, for God will not leave you hopeless.

Let me say that if you have suffered great loss in your life, I do not believe that your life will be the same as it was before your loss. How can it be? The loss of a loved one can create significant, permanent changes for us. One change is certain: the person who has passed on can no longer be here with us, in physical form. That alone is a profound change to have to cope with.

But there can be a myriad of other changes that necessarily attach themselves to a loss. The changes can range from being emotional in nature to practical. For example, when a person loses a loved one, they are often forced to play new and different roles in their life and in the lives of others. Some people are faced with single parenthood. Some need to become more self-sufficient such as learning new skills in the area of finance or home improvement. Regardless of what challenges our loss has brought to our lives, we can be assured that these difficult and painful events will impact us. It is what *we do* with these significant events, however, that will make or break us.

This difficult lesson was driven home to me by watching my brother Vinnie's last months on this earth and learning of his death. After Jeanne died, my family and I mourned her loss. Some mourned for her even prior to her dying, anticipating her passing. Even Jeanne grieved her circumstances as she battled the cancer in her body. All of these things seemed quite normal and expected considering the circumstances. What my family and I noticed though, after Jeanne's passing, was a very unique response from my brother Vinnie. I cannot speak for Vinnie, because no person can fully know what is in another person's heart. But if observing a person's behavior and listening to his words indicates anything, Vinnie showed us what was in his heart.

Let me begin by saying that my brother was a wonderful, committed Christian man. He had his faults and quirks, as we all do, but he had a heart of gold. He loved what was good and hated what was evil and struggled to make that a reality in his journey on this earth. Vinnie had a true faith in Jesus Christ as his Savior, the redeemer of his sins. But Jesus is so much more than that. Jesus wants to be Lord of our lives, which means that we give Him pre-eminence over every area of our lives. *Especially* when our hearts are broken. I believe that Vinnie could not see his way to trusting Jesus for this great need that he had in the months before his death.

Upon listening to my brother in the weeks and months follow-ing Jeanne's death, I could see that he was in a deeper, darker state of despair than anyone else in my family. We were all hurt-ing, but we were able, even in our early days of mourning, to derive some sense of comfort and strength from each other and from our faith. I did not see that with Vinnie. This should not be taken as a criticism, but just as the observation that it is.

---

## I tell you that you can find comfort in Jesus.

---

Perhaps you are in the same condition that Vinnie was in right after losing his twin sister. Maybe you can't seem to find any solace at all in your circumstances. I tell you that you can find comfort in Jesus. Isaiah rightly prophesied years before the coming of Christ that Jesus would come to bring not only salva-tion, but comfort and healing. "He has sent me to bind up the brokenhearted... to comfort all who mourn, and provide for those who grieve—to bestow on them a crown of beauty for ashes, the oil of gladness instead of mourning, and a garment of praise instead of a spirit of despair" (Isaiah 61: 1, 3).

It is perfectly normal to mourn the loss of a loved one. God made us emotional beings with the ability to experience all emotions, even sadness. The Bible says that Jesus was deeply moved and even wept upon learning of the death of His friend Lazarus and upon seeing all of the mourning going on around Him (John 11: 33-35). But sometimes we can allow our circum-stances to overcome us, our intense feelings to overtake us. This is where we can go wrong.

Our shoulders were not made to carry the heavy burdens that tragedy can bring. We were meant to fulfill the normal responsibilities in our lives, but we were not meant to endure life's hardships alone. We need to look to the Lord Jesus for our help. The Lord says in Matthew 11: 28, "Come to me, all you who are weary and burdened, and I will give you rest." What a wonderful invitation! Jesus is inviting us all to come to Him, so that He can give us His peace.

A wound needs the proper medication to heal. The healing that we *all* need is the healing from above. And only Jesus, the Prince of Peace, can give it to us. Along with His peace, He can give us His wisdom so we can see all things in a heavenly way and not in a human way. I have taken great comfort as I have hung onto the words of Jesus. When you just don't know how you will get through, meditate and hang on to the only true source of comfort—the truth, the Word of God. This can carry you through.

I wish that my brother Vinnie could have hung on and held fast to the Word as a source of healing for his soul, for his broken heart. Especially since he was a believer in the Faith. I believe that Vinnie's emotional brokenheartedness ultimately lead to the physical death of his heart, which took his life.

Sadly though, Vinnie is not a rare case. Many people, even believers, either don't seek help at all or look for help in the wrong places. I challenge you today to learn something from this tragic story. Don't allow your circumstances to take your very life away. You may be alive in body but dead in your heart and emotions. You may be storing up so much pain in your heart that you wish you were physically dead. I know how it can be, I have been there. I was filled with so much sadness that, though I was alive, for a while I was paralyzed from "living."

Just know that it can be different for you. God wants it to be different for you. "For I know the plans I have for you," declares the Lord, "plans to prosper you and not to harm you, plans to give you hope and a future. Then you will call upon me and come and pray to me, and I will listen to you. You will seek me and find me when you seek me with all your heart" (Jeremiah 29: 11-13). Notice that God has a promise to prosper you and give you hope and a future. But with that promise comes a condition. You must call upon Him, pray to Him, and seek Him. Cry out to the Lord and let Him heal your heart.

As you meditate on His Word, you will learn how much He cares for you and wants to bind up your wounds. I pray that as you read about our Great Physician in the Bible, you will trust in Him for all your needs.

It bears repeating that experiencing emotional pain, sorrow, and grief after losing a loved one is a normal, natural part of being human. It can be particularly difficult the first and second year following a person's death. Remembering birthdays and anniversaries and going through holidays without that person can be extremely painful. The losses I have suffered are very real and ever-present in my life. I still feel pain and have a place of emptiness in my heart for my sister Jeanne and brother Vinnie. I suspect I always will. But I am learning to lean on God for my strength, my hope, my peace, and my comfort. I am beginning to live again in Him. I see that *joy really does come in the morning*, if you put yourself in a position to receive God's healing touch in your life.

Being in the midst of tragedy does not mean that God has separated Himself from us. "Be strong and courageous. Do not be afraid or terrified because of them, for the Lord your God goes with you; he will never leave you nor forsake you" (Deuteronomy 31: 6). While we may feel frightened, we need to remember that God does not abandon us, even if *we* walk away from Him for a time. If you are experiencing an emotional "wilderness," God can refresh you even there. It is in a dry desert that water tastes the best. It is only in the darkness that you can see even a small flicker of light. You can sit at the Lord's feet and receive the rest and consolation that you need. He has rivers of living waters for you, even in the driest desert. He wants to do a new thing for you, if you will let Him.

If you have been in a place where you have not been able to receive even a small amount of comfort and peace, if you have been stuck in despair for a while, meditate on the words to the song "My Life is in Your Hands," sung by the Christian artist Mr. Kirk Franklin. I have heard it sung at my church a few times. At first, I cried because I could not imagine that it could be for me. Now when I hear it, I sing with joy and confidence, having experienced first-hand God's peace and healing in the midst of tragedy. Here are some of the lyrics:

> *You don't have to worry and don't you be afraid.*
> *Joy comes in the morning, troubles they don't last always.*
> *For there's a friend named Jesus who will wipe*
>     *your tears away.*
> *And if your heart is broken, just lift your hands and say.*
>
> *CHORUS: Oh! I know that I can make it.*
> *I know that I can stand.*
> *No matter what may come my way,*
> *My life is in your hands.*
>
> *With Jesus I can take it,*
> *With Him I know I can stand.*
> *No matter what may come my way,*
> *My life is in your hands.*

Whatever your situation, I want to encourage you: Don't give up! If you can just hang in there, you will see that though there is weeping, joy really does come again.

# Chapter Two

# Living Again

After I emerged from what seemed like an emotionally cata-
tonic state during the months following my brother's
death, I was faced with a choice. I had the choice to live with
spirit and purpose or to "live as the living dead." I saw the
emotional anguish my brother Vinnie was in after Jeanne's
death. I saw how he just could not break free from the pain and
sadness which he felt from her passing. I eventually saw the
devastating toll that this bondage took on my brother's life. It
not only took his life, but wreaked utter havoc in the lives of my
family and me. Now after losing Vinnie too, I was faced with
making the decision of how I would live out the rest of my life.

I was not in emotional bondage after Jeanne's death, but I felt
darn close to it after Vinnie's. I think I began to know how Vinnie
was feeling right before he died, because now I felt desperate
and hopeless. I went about my daily responsibilities only
because my children, husband, and extended family were
counting on me; but my joy was gone. My sister-in-law has
since told me that when we would speak in the months follow-

ing Vinnie's death, I had a mechanical, lifeless monotone to my voice. That is exactly how I felt inside. In short, I felt my purpose for living slipping away from me, and I was scared. I felt like I was dying from the inside out. I felt empty. Frankly, there were times when I did not want to be here anymore. When I wasn't feeling numb and empty, I felt pain. I wasn't interested in living like that, and at the time, I wasn't sure that it would ever change. Where did *my* faith in God go?

I did not want what happened to Vinnie to happen to me. I believe that Vinnie did the best he could; he just could not find his way out of his pain. I knew that if I continued in this downward spiral of negative emotions, I would be digging a pit for myself that would eventually be too deep for me to get out of. What happened to Vinnie could just as well happen to me. I decided I wanted something different—I decided I wanted to live again!

---

**You have the right to live! You have the right to be here, even though your loved one is not.**

---

Once you *decide* to live again, you can begin the process. You first have to make the choice. If you have been unable to face making this decision, or if you have decided to live in body only, pay careful attention to this. *You have the right to live! You have the right to be here, even though your loved one is not.* Whatever the circumstances surrounding your loss, it is still okay for *you* to live. In Deuteronomy 30: 19, 20, God is speaking to the Israelites and says, "This day I call heaven and earth as witnesses against you that I have set before you life and death, blessings and curses.

Now choose life, so that you and your children may live and that you may love the Lord your God, listen to his voice, and hold fast to him. For the Lord is your life, and he will give you many years in the land he swore to give to your fathers, Abraham, Isaac and Jacob." God tells us that we can have life or death; in case we need help making the right choice, He tells us to choose life. It is not just *okay* for us to go on living, but we *should* go on living.

I remember feeling very guilty when I would experience a glimmer of happiness in the course of my day after Jeanne and Vinnie died. I thought that it was being disrespectful to my sister's and brother's memory. I also thought that I did not have the *right* to feel happy again. I would actually catch myself laughing or enjoying time with someone and stop myself. After all, what kind of a sister would I be if I felt joy while Jeanne and Vinnie lay dead? (I speak only of their bodies, because I believe that their souls and spirits are with our Father in Heaven.) But then I realized that this attitude would not help Jeanne and Vinnie and only served as an obstacle to my happiness. It would just create more loss.

I began to understand that the length and depth of my grief was not necessarily a direct reflection of my love for my brother and sister. My love for them is immeasurable; they will always be in my heart. Nothing can ever change that. Likewise, no amount or intensity of grieving will define my love for them. Besides, choosing to live after losing Jeanne and Vinnie has not precluded me from grieving for them. You can grieve your loss and still carry on with the business of living. Additionally, there really is nothing I can do for them now. Jeanne and Vinnie made their choices in life, which determined their eternal resting places. I have peace that they are both with God—there is no better place to be!

Thinking that it is disrespectful or shameful to live with spirit and purpose after the loss of a loved one is simply wrong. One has no correlation with the other. In fact, I dare say that most, if not all, of our loved ones who have left this world would be angry with us if they knew that we stopped living because of them.

We have an obligation to fulfill the purpose for our lives on this earth. We have been given gifts and talents to use for the good of others. We are cheating God, others, and ourselves if we don't live our lives out as God intended. Every person will experience good and bad, happy and sad times while living on this earth. We cannot allow tragic events to devour our very lives. We might allow it for a time and certainly mourn the pain of our losses, but ultimately, it is our own choice whether or not we will rise above the pain and permit ourselves to live again. Even when we don't understand everything that happens in our lives and are perhaps angry about some of these things, the Bible instructs us to put our trust in the One who really does know best:

> There is a time for everything,
> and a season for every activity under heaven:
> a time to be born and a time to die,
> a time to plant and a time to uproot,
> a time to kill and a time to heal,
> a time to tear down and a time to build,
> a time to weep and a time to laugh,
> a time to mourn and a time to dance,
> a time to scatter stones and a time to gather them,
> a time to embrace and a time to refrain,
> a time to search and a time to give up,
> a time to keep and a time to throw away,

*a time to tear and a time to mend,*
*a time to be silent and a time to speak,*
*a time to love and a time to hate,*
*a time for war and a time for peace.*

Ecclesiastes 3: 1 - 8

I know how scary it can be to try living again. We need to take baby steps as we begin the process—even baby steps can be scary, but we must start somewhere. Perhaps a good place to start is by going to a trusted friend's house for a quiet dinner.

About one month after Vinnie died, it was my husband's birthday. I remember being invited to my in-laws' home for a small celebration. It was very hard for me to even think about going. I so wanted to honor my husband for his birthday, but I just did not feel that I had it in me to be in the company of others, even if it was family that I loved. I remember telling my husband and mother-in-law that I was sorry; I wanted them to go through with the birthday dinner, but I simply could not go. I felt that I was in no condition emotionally, and I did not want to ruin everyone else's good time.

They both persuaded me to go, telling me that it would not be the same without me and that it would do me good to get out a little. They were right. I had to stop at the cemetery first though—I just had to. After spending some time alone at the grave sites, I felt a release, and in the end, I actually did enjoy that little birthday party.

My husband helped me by taking me for a short walk every evening after dinner. Sometimes we would talk and sometimes we wouldn't—we were just doing something together, and that was what was important.

Having at least one or two people you can go to for support can be very healing. It is so important to be able to express your thoughts *and* feelings in a "safe" environment. That is, where you won't be judged. The grieving process is very personal and individual. Aside from being destructive, which is clearly unacceptable, there is no right or wrong way to grieve.

I have had many open dialogues with family and friends that have proved very therapeutic. Just be careful who you go to and what you say. Not everyone is in a place where they can give you what you need, and that can at times create more pain for you. You may be expecting a great show of support from someone who has been in close relationship with you, but you may get very little. A casual acquaintance may offer more empathy for your situation than someone you've known for years. You may hear things like, "You just have to move on," and wonder if the person is right or just very insensitive.

Understand that many people are very uncomfortable "dealing with" someone in mourning. They may be afraid to say the wrong thing, so they say nothing and avoid you. They may be so anxious to help you out of your pain that they say inappropriate things that only perpetuate the pain. In the end, helpful or not, most people mean well.

I pray that you will first make the decision to truly live again, with spirit and purpose for your life! Later on in this book, I discuss in greater detail *how* to really live again. Through these and other constructive suggestions, I know that you too can find your way. Be encouraged by God's Word when He says, "My grace is sufficient for you, for my power is made perfect in weakness" (2 Corinthians 12: 9). Remember, God is calling you to *life*, and those whom He calls, He also equips.

## Chapter Three

# Love One Another

We are ready to move on to examine a powerful lesson, one that I was faced with learning as a result of losing my brother and sister. It is a lesson about love. After the twins died, I remember asking myself, "Did I love them while they were here? I mean *really* love them! How could I have done better? Do I truly show love for my family and others now? What really is love?" After much prayer time and searching the Word of God, I was reminded of the following. Worldly love is loving someone *because of* who they are. The God-kind of love, or agape love, is loving someone *despite* who they are. The difference is obvious: worldly love is based on certain conditions, and agape love is unconditional.

No one has ever walked in perfect agape love at all times, except for Jesus Christ Himself. Yet, we are commanded to do so, no matter what the price. Jesus said, "A new command I give you: Love one another. As I have loved you, so you must love one another" (John 13: 34). We see that we are not only commanded to love, but to love as Jesus did, unconditionally.

You may be saying to yourself, "I love my family unconditionally. After all, I do so much for them." You might think that your willingness to die for a loved one, dive in front of a speeding truck for them, or even take that terminal disease and put it on yourself if you could is unconditional love. I say that these instances would be expressions of *sacrificial* love. And I would venture to guess that many of us would be willing to lay down our lives for someone else, especially for our children. But I tell you that this is not necessarily unconditional love.

Consider this question. Why do we have trouble accepting people who are different from us? I am not even speaking of outright prejudice—that is, disapproving of a person because of their race, skin color, gender, ethnicity and the like. While this obvious form of prejudice is wrong, I am speaking of accepting people in our neighborhoods, schools, churches, and even our own families when they don't exactly march to the beat of our drummer.

**When our approval and acceptance of a person is based on how closely their life mirrors ours, our love for them is very conditional.**

When our approval and acceptance of a person is based on how closely their life mirrors ours, our love for them is very conditional. I am not referring here to accepting sinful lifestyles. Often, people choose paths for their lives that prove to be harmful to themselves and others. Some even choose sinful lifestyles that we cannot and should not condone. But Jesus did say in Jude 23 that we should hate the sin but love the sinner. A person's sin should not disable us from truly loving and valuing that person as a human being.

If we reflect on the story of the prodigal son, we see that after his son who had gone astray returned home with a repentant heart, the father "was filled with compassion for him; he ran to his son, threw his arms around him and kissed him." (Luke 15: 11 - 32) What a beautiful picture of how Father God treats us after we return to Him with a repentant heart. Truly forgiving someone is a powerful form of love.

We may say that we forgive, but do we really? Do we offer forgiveness to a person only after we have rubbed their noses in their error, treating them for a time like they are subservient to us because of their actions? No where in the story of the prodigal son did the father have that attitude. The story serves as a model of the kind of forgiving attitude that we should have towards one another.

Do we forgive the offenses of others but still keep a running tab of their mistakes for future reference? This has been a pitfall for me. I could easily forgive someone who hurt me, but I could not seem to forget the offense. I would replay the situation in my mind, over and over again. Not only is that not forgiveness, but it is a form of bondage. Here is what God has to say about it. In Psalm 103: 9 - 12, David inspired by the Holy Spirit writes, "He will not always accuse, nor will he harbor his anger forever; he does not treat us as our sins deserve or repay us according to our iniquities. For as high as the heavens are above the earth, so great is his love for those who fear him; as far as the east is from the west, so far has he removed our transgressions from us." Also, in Isaiah 43: 25, we read, "I, even I, am he who blots out your transgressions, for my own sake, and remembers your sins no more." When I grasped this concept and began to live it, it really freed me up inside.

God not only removes our sin far away from us, but He

remembers it no more. We should do likewise. In practical terms, this means we are not only to forgive, but we are not to bring up the offense again. When thoughts that conveniently remind us of past hurts pop into our minds, we need to consciously push them out of our minds. Even if someone who has hurt us does not have a repentant heart, as can often be the case, we are still commanded to love them. We don't have to approve of or accept someone's sin, but we are instructed to forgive when necessary and love at all times.

The story of the prodigal son is one example of love, but what about others? What if there is no sin involved? What if the differences between people lie in personalities, ideas, tastes, temperaments, chosen paths and the like? Where does love come into play in these situations? Consider these questions: Do we really value the people in our lives as we ought, despite our differences? Does the measure of worth that we apportion to others hinge on the degree of likeness between us?

If we are truly honest with ourselves, I think we would all agree that, at least to some degree, we are more apt to give credence to someone who is more like us. It is inherently comfortable and self-assuring to do this because it affirms our choices and who we are. I know I feel better being around people like myself. But it is precisely here, when faced with the challenge of relating to people who are different from us, that we are given opportunities to demonstrate love.

I have two young children. As they grow, I am observing the similarities and differences between us. I am also noticing something about myself. That is, I can more easily deal with the attributes in my children that I understand and identify with versus those that I do not understand. For example, when my daughter, Ashley, is expressing a sensitivity towards a particular issue that I too am or was sensitive to, I find that I am usually very patient and effective in helping her deal with that issue. If, on the other hand, she expresses a sensitivity or concern about something and I don't share that same concern, I may not be as sensitive or helpful to her. Why? Because I am having trouble relating to her.

Learning to identify with her sensitivities is a way I can demonstrate my love for her. This does not mean that I need to feel and think everything that she feels and thinks. Rather, I should be cultivating a richer understanding for what makes my daughter tick, and I should be more available for her in terms of communication, empathy, and perhaps needed guidance. I believe that this concept is where the saying "walk a mile in another man's shoes" came from.

Recently, Ashley asked if she could play soccer in the town league with the other girls her age. My husband and I readily agreed, as we both played and enjoyed sports as kids ourselves. We registered her, got all the equipment she would need, and excitedly brought her to her first practice. She so enjoyed it and really did very well. The coaches felt she had real potential. A week later, we went to watch Ashley play her first game of organized soccer. Randy, Christian, and I got to the field and took our seats along the sidelines of the soccer field. At first, it was wonderful. Our little Ashley was running up and down that field, kicking that soccer ball, and really doing beautifully. She looked like she was having a lot of fun, and we could not have been happier. As she ran ahead of the pack of girls scurrying for the ball, close to scoring a goal, I was cheering, "Go 'Ashey,' go! Go! Go! Go!" Any proud parent knows the thrill of watching your child participate in something constructive that they really enjoy. But the thrill did not last.

Suddenly, Ashley came off the field crying, saying that she was having trouble breathing. We figured that she was just a bit winded from all the running she was doing, so we let her sit out a while. When she caught her breath, she went back into the game, but it wasn't long before she got winded again and subsequently got very upset. She did not want to play anymore. She sat out the rest of the game, but insisted that she did not want to play soccer anymore. We took her home and tried to explain to her that getting tired and winded after running was very normal, but if she took regular intervals of rest, she would be fine. We tried to explain that the more she practiced her running, the more stamina she would develop. We tried every form of logic, but still she insisted that she did not want to play. Clearly, she was very upset by the whole situation.

We dropped the subject until the next week, when it was time for the next soccer game. Reluctantly, Ashley agreed to go to the field. She practiced with her team, but when it came time for the regular game to start, she panicked and refused to play. I really became angry with her because I felt she was being unreasonable and maybe even lazy. After all, she seemed to be having a good time when she was playing, and she was really quite good at soccer. So what was the problem?

When I decided to put aside the expectations I had of Ashley playing soccer and chose to really listen empathetically, I found out what the problem was. In the months just prior to Ashley playing soccer, our son Christian had begun experiencing asthmatic attacks. Before the situation had come under control, Ashley had become well acquainted with middle-of-the-night runs to the emergency room because her brother was in respiratory distress. I'm sure it was frightening for her to be yanked out of bed in the wee hours of the morning and raced to the hospital with a set of very concerned and anxious parents and a baby brother who was having trouble breathing. Need I say more?

Ashley explained to us that when she gets winded playing

soccer, she gets worried that she won't be able to breathe, just like her baby brother. We assured her that being a little short of breath is completely different than having an asthmatic attack and that she did not have asthma. I tried to calm her fears by checking her lung sounds with my stethoscope and reassuring her that everything was fine. That still did not help. She did not mind practicing with her team, but she did not want to play in the games. Practicing did not require as much running as the real game did. When the coaches offered her to play the position of goalie, she refused, knowing that it would be unfair for only her to play goalie and not allow the other girls a chance at the position.

The soccer season came and went and Ashley did not play another game. My husband and I were disappointed, but at least we knew why Ashley did not want to play anymore. We listened to her with our ears *and* our hearts. Though at some point in this whole scenario, I am sure we did not handle the situation with all the patience and understanding that we should have, ultimately we found our way. We did not like the final outcome, but we felt that forcing our daughter to do something that she was frightened to do would be harmful to her. More importantly, I think Ashley felt heard. We asked her what she was feeling inside that made her protest so strongly, she told us, and we listened and respected her wishes.

When I stop for just a few moments and try to see things from her little eyes and not limit myself to only my perspective, things go so much better. I sense that my daughter feels loved in those moments because I am valuing her thoughts, feelings, and perspectives. This illustration has to do with a small problem and a small child. But as our families grow, problems can grow. Why? Because children grow into adolescents, and adolescents grow into adults. As individuals become "their own people," differences emerge between them, even within families. When we don't know how to handle these differences, our relationships become strained, complicated and sometimes even scary. We can minimize the complications by seeking to understand each other without assigning value judgments.

Sincerely listening to another with an open heart requires that we lay aside our preconceived notions and open ourselves to possibly hearing something different than what agrees with our perspective. It challenges us to look beyond ourselves and the little worlds that we have created, with their protective walls, and explore another's thoughts. That can make a lot of people uncomfortable.

---

**Respecting another's thoughts
and feelings is a demonstration
of love.**

---

I must emphasize that I am not suggesting that you consider choosing a sinful lifestyle or behavior in the name of "being open" to alternative perspectives. We must hold strong to the fundamental beliefs that we know to be rightly aligned with the Word of God. The Bible tells us in Ephesians 4: 15 to "... speak the truth in love..." even if it goes against whatever the popular culture of the day is. I am referring to non-moral and non-ethical issues such as academic and professional pursuits, life dreams, and personal inner feelings or conflicts, to name a few. When we can really listen to someone who is allowing themselves to be vulnerable with us by opening up their heart, we demonstrate love. We create an environment of security, trust, and safety so that this person knows he or she can come to us with anything, without fear of reproach, because we will listen without judging.

The idea of respect naturally flows out of love. Respecting another's thoughts and feelings is a demonstration of love. Feelings are not right or wrong; they are just feelings. What we do with those feelings can be right or wrong, but the feelings themselves cannot be. Offering respect to your loved ones is a tremendous gift. My sister Jeanne was always speaking of respect. She was a school teacher in the junior high school that she attended herself as a youth and, evidently, heavily stressed the concept of showing respect for others. At the eighth grade graduation ceremony, just a month and a half after Jeanne died, some of her students sang a song dedicated to their beloved teacher, Miss Lo Iacono. It was no surprise that the song they chose was "Respect," by Aretha Franklin. Jeanne both showed respect to her students and expected to receive it. She obviously made a strong impression on the children and on me. I was very proud of her that day.

When a person faces criticism after revealing a part of themselves to another, it can really destroy a part of that person's self-esteem. It also breaches whatever level of trust there may have been between those two people. It is no longer "safe" to be truly honest with that individual. Why not consider taking a more understanding, sensitive, and respectful approach when relating to your loved ones? Then, if our children are in need of a confidante, they will be more likely to choose us instead of a misguided friend. And remember, when guidance or correction is called for, let us speak the truth in love.

Several years ago, I was leaving a job to join a practice which held more opportunity for me. As a physical therapist, I always enjoy cultivating warm and friendly relationships with my patients where possible. When the staff and patients heard I was leaving, they planned a surprise party to wish me well. Everyone brought thoughtful gifts and parlayed sweet sentiments. One of my patients gave me a mug that read, "Congratulations, from the folks who know you best... and like you anyway." I thought to myself, "Wow, this guy knows me better than I thought." I am sure that this patient was just trying to be funny; after all, we had become friends. But we can learn something from the sentiment on the mug. At times, it is hard to love the people that we live with because we know them the best. We know their quirks, faults, rough spots, weaknesses, idiosyncrasies and all-around "push-buttons"; and we all have them.

Ephesians 4:2 tells us, "Be completely humble and gentle; be patient, bearing with one another in love." God is instructing us to bear with one another in love because it is not in our natures to do so. Often times, we love others with the expectation of getting something in return. When we do not get the desired response from our "loving" actions or even get lashed out at with a negative response, we might seek to retrieve our love. Indeed, that is not love at all, but a self-serving attitude concealed in a cloak of love. True loving is giving love because you want to minister to the needs of another person (even when they are acting unlovable)... period! I do not purport to have a corner on this market. But, while bearing with one another can, at times, be extremely challenging, God wants to help us. "The one who calls you is faithful and he will do it" (I Thessalonians 5: 24). God doesn't ask us to do anything that He doesn't equip us for.

I remember a time as a young girl having done something wrong, though I do not recall now what I had actually done. What I do remember is being very hard on myself because of my mistake. I couldn't forgive myself. I further recall telling my brother Vinnie about it. His response has stuck with me through all of these years, and I suspect it always will. He said to me, "It's okay Fran, you just made a mistake. You don't have to be so hard on yourself. Just try to do better next time." Vinnie's words broke through any harsh wall of punishment I was building for myself. I truly felt forgiveness, and I learned that it was okay to "be human." God stills loves us.

This truth is made obvious in Romans 5: 8: "But God demonstrated his own love for us in this: While we were still sinners, Christ died for us." In addition, 1 John 1: 9 says, "If we confess our sins, he is faithful and just and will forgive us our sins and purify us from all unrighteousness." Vinnie demonstrated patience with me and was bearing with me in love. It is funny how the times that we might otherwise consider fleeting, insignificant moments in our lives can stay with us. This short-lived moment was not insignificant or fleeting at all. I am grateful for my brother's loving heart. Now, if I find myself in error again, I remember Vinnie's words. I ask for forgiveness, let go of the shame, and move on with the business of living, hopefully having learned something new from the experience. Further I try to be mindful of the love that I was shown so that I can do likewise for someone else.

What of the "good stuff" that makes up the important people in our life? Why do we seem to focus on the negative with such clarity and pass right over the positive qualities? If you are not one of those people who do this, congratulations. Unfortunately, you are in the minority. Most of us are nicer to and more patient with strangers than members of our own family.

I think this propensity to focus on the negative is simply part of the human condition; nevertheless, we are commanded to do differently: "But now you must rid yourselves of all such things as these: anger, rage, malice, slander and filthy language from your lips" (Colossians 3: 8). In the book of Ephesians 4: 29, Paul writes, "Do not let any unwholesome talk come out of your mouths, but only what is helpful for building others up according to their needs, that it may benefit those who listen." When we criticize, judge, and remind a person of their faults, we are using our lips in a slanderous and malicious way, and that does not benefit anyone. Remember when your mother said, "If you can't say something nice, don't say anything at all"? She was right! She understood how negative, critical words only serve to tear a person down. We need to concentrate our efforts on building our loved ones up rather than tearing them down.

## Why do we save our heartfelt thoughts about a person for their funeral?

During the time of my sister's and brother's funerals, and the months subsequent to them, I remember so many people, including my family and me, saying wonderful things about my siblings. Every good quality that they ever demonstrated in their lives was brought to light. Only the kindest of sentiments were exchanged and the saddest of tears shed at the passing of these two young people. We cried for ourselves, wondering how we would go on with our lives without them. I believe that these exchanges were indeed sincere. But as I observed and participated in this, I wondered to myself, "Why didn't we say these things to them (with the same intensity and with more frequency) when they were still with us? Why do we save our heartfelt thoughts about a person for their funeral?"

You may be a person who does express love, support, and gratitude to your loved ones. My family and I are certainly not without our moments of expressing loving kindness to each other. But let's face it, most of us could do a lot better in this department. If you admire or appreciate someone, why not tell them so right now? Don't assume that they know just because of a particular relationship you have with them. If you love someone, why not show them with any number of many expressions of love. For example, spend time with someone, listen to someone, hug someone, tell someone you love them, or tell someone how special they really are to you. The possibilities are endless.

The Bible tells us in Proverbs 3: 27, 28, "Do not withhold good from those who deserve it, when it is in your power to act. Do not say to your neighbor, 'Come back later; I'll give it tomorrow'—when you now have it with you." Further, the Bible says, "Do not boast about tomorrow, for you do not know what a day may bring forth" (Proverbs 27: 1). I learned that lesson the hard way when I got the call that Vinnie had passed away. Vinnie and I had spoken just six days prior to his death. He was seemingly healthy and was looking forward to starting a new job that week. All seemed well. Six days after our conversation, without warning, he was gone.

I pose the same questions to you that I asked myself at the beginning of this chapter. Do you *really* love the people closest to you? Do your actions towards your loved ones reflect what you say you feel for them? We do not know what a day may bring forth; therefore, let us take every opportunity to show our love for one another. What are we waiting for? The only opportunity you have to do something is right now. We are not guaranteed a tomorrow, and good intentions won't amount to much if your loved one doesn't know that they really, really matter to you. There are no second chances after a person dies. Once a person is gone, so are your opportunities to show your love directly to them. Find the good in the people you say you love, then tell them about it. Try to overlook the bad. Since our tragedies, my family has learned to say "I love you" right after we say "good-bye" to each other. If you love someone, go the extra mile to show them, not just in word, but also in deed.

*Chapter Four*

# Don't Put Off Today

Most of you are familiar with the saying, "Don't put off till tomorrow what you can do today." These words never rang more true to me than after losing my brother and sister. Anyone who has lost a loved one understands that there are no second chances to do what you always wanted or intended to do for someone, after that someone leaves this earth. This is why it is so very important to *carpe diem*, or seize the day!

It is truly a sad sight to see people cry over what might have been—that is, words that never got spoken, events that never took place, or hearts that never got reconciled. I believe that these and similar issues that go unresolved are what heavily contributes to feelings of depression and despair in someone who is grieving. It is difficult enough to mourn the actual loss of the person, but to have to mourn the loss of what you could have done for or been to that person adds a heavy burden to an already weighty load.

You will recall from chapter three that in the book of Proverbs, God instructs us as follows: 1) do good to others, when it is in your power to act, and 2) we do not know what a day may bring forth. We should seize every opportunity to do good and serve others. The Bible tells us in Galatians 6: 9, "Let us not become weary in doing good, for at the proper time we will reap a harvest if we do not give up." There are many benefits to be reaped by following this truth. One benefit though is having peace in your heart, knowing that you did all you could for your loved ones while they were still with you. Remember, sometimes there are no second chances.

---

**It is difficult enough to mourn the actual loss of the person, but to have to mourn the loss of what you could have done for or been to that person, adds a heavy burden to an already weighty load.**

---

Making happy memories for yourself and loved ones is a great way to seize the day. Whether we realize it or not, we all make memories with our actions and our choices. Some memories will be good and some not so good. Why not purpose in your heart to make a happy memory for you and a loved one today. Plan a picnic lunch or an outing to the beach with family or friends. If you have children, try to make some special time with each child on a regular basis. I know a family with seven kids, and naturally, the parents' time is spread very thin. To compensate for their inability to give a lot of one-on-one attention to each child, one of the parents tries to allocate two hours a week, alone, with one of the children. One child, every week, gets two hours of undivided attention, from one of his parents. It makes the children feel very special, when it's their week.

You don't have to spend a lot of money. Just give a bit of time and a bit of yourself. You can take a bike ride with him, have breakfast with her, shop, bake, hike or do whatever you both like. The idea is to spend time together, creating an opportunity to talk, listen, have fun, and just be with each other. Spending time can create such intimacy between two people because you are valuing the other person enough to spend your time with him or her.

I remember many family vacations growing up. Many happy and funny memories were created during these times. Of course, there were some very trying and tense moments, but those difficult moments invariably turned into funny stories years later. Take, for example, my family's car trip from New Jersey to Florida. I still don't understand how or why my parents would venture to take five young children down the east coast of the United States in a station wagon. They did, though, and lived to tell about it, so now I pass the story along to you.

All seven of us were packed and ready to drive to Miami Beach to visit my grandparents for one of the holidays. My parents were in the front seat with coolers and bags filled with supplies sandwiched between them. Three of us kids sat in the back seat, sniping and poking each other, fighting over who would sit by the door at the next rest stop. The remaining two kids were in the rear portion of the wagon, probably making faces at the car behind us. Finally, strapped to the roof of the car was all of our luggage, which my father had painstakingly secured himself. My brother Vinnie was one of the kids sitting in the rear end of the wagon. Vinnie was also at an age in which he had the propensity to tell tall tales. As he looked out the rear window to count the lines that passed beneath the car's wheels, he began to holler, "Dad! Dad! The suitcases fell off the roof!" My parents, weary of Vinnie's lying, yelled back, "If you don't stop telling lies, we're going to have to punish you." Vinnie continued, "But Dad.......!" At that, my father glanced into the rear view mirror only to see the family's underwear strewn across Interstate 95. My father pulled over and ran down the highway, dodging on-coming traffic to recover what was left of our underwear. This was not very funny at the time, but it is hilarious when we all think about it now. We would not have this funny memory if my parents had not gone to the effort of taking us on that trip.

Even as we kids got older, we went away on vacation as a family. We learned of a great card game called Pounce. It is like a giant game of solitaire that requires at least four players, and each player has his own deck of cards. The game is fast-moving, action-packed, and a lot of fun. With seven people playing, you could imagine the noise that came forth. Playing this game, though, could easily try a person's patience and often caused tense, competitive feelings amongst us players. Almost without fail, this is how our night would unfold. It would be sometime around midnight. Jeanne would quit early and go to bed exhausted and frustrated. We would all urge her to continue to play with us, but she would just throw her hands up, rejecting our offer. After accepting her refusal to play, the rest of us would just begin to play another round without her.

About two hands later, Jeanne would emerge from the bedroom in disgust, saying, "All right, deal me in!" She really did not want to play anymore, but she did not want to miss out on the activity. It was like something was drawing her to the card table that she simply could not resist. Certainly it was not the hollering, the bickering, or the junk food. It likely was the sense of belonging that she enjoyed, even if it was to a nutty family. We had come to expect that Jeanne would go through this routine of quitting, then coming back, so we would leave her seat open and have a snack waiting for her when she returned.

These are the times that are precious, that you can treasure in your heart. No matter what happens, no one can take them from you. But in order for you to have these memories, you first have to make them. I don't recall going to very fancy places—my family did not have an exorbitant amount of money to spend. But we did not need a lot of money to have fun, and neither do you. We were very happy with the simple things. Since the twins have passed away, my parents have remarked several times how happy they are that we took family vacations and made time to make our own memories. When you get right down to it, memories and maybe some pictures are all you really have to hold on to after a loved one passes. Don't miss your chance to cultivate wonderful memories with the people you love.

The term carpe diem does not apply only to taking opportunities or making happy memories. It can also be applied to that important concept of forgiveness. Forgiveness is an amazing thing. There is so much power in forgiveness—in particular, the power to set free. Conversely, there is a lot of power in unforgiveness—that is, the power to hold captive. I believe that my sister Jeanne was aware of this truth because before she died, she had made peace with most, if not all, of the key people in her life. It was truly a comfort to know that there was nothing ugly or unresolved between my sister and me and, as far as I know, between my brother and me.

It is tragic to see people come to a funeral for someone that they were fighting with or perhaps had not been on speaking terms with because of some quarrel or misunderstanding. Life is short! Even if you live 120 years, in the scope of eternity, your life is still short. This is not a dress rehearsal, it's the real thing.

We do not get another chance at living our lives here on this earth after we die. So when it comes to relationships with people and the issues that concern us, it is important to ask ourselves the question, "How important is this matter, in the big scheme of things?" I am not suggesting that we should be doormats for other people. I believe in setting healthy boundaries in relationships. I just think that sometimes people can get so stuck in an issue because of principle that, in the interim, they lose the people and the relationships involved.

---

**We do not get another chance at living our lives here on this earth after we die.**

---

God speaks to us of forgiveness throughout the Bible. First and foremost, the Bible tells us, "If we confess our sins, he is faithful and just and will forgive us our sins and purify us from all unrighteousness" (1 John 1: 9). This piece of scripture obviously applies to our need for forgiveness from God. But God also clearly instructs us a myriad of times to forgive others as well as to seek the forgiveness of others where it is necessary: "Bear with each other and forgive whatever grievances you may have against one another. Forgive as the Lord forgave you" (Colossians 3: 13). The Bible further explains, "Therefore, if you are offering your gift at the altar and there remember that your brother has something against you, leave your gift there in front of the altar. First go and be reconciled to your brother; then come and offer your gift" (Matthew 5: 23, 24). These can be tough scriptures to read and follow because all of us, at one time or another, have encountered people in our lives that have hurt us or made life difficult for us. Forgiveness is probably not the first thing that comes to mind when you think of someone who has caused you trouble. I know it is not usually for me. Similarly, seeking forgiveness can be a difficult and humbling experience. Yet we are called to walk in these two principles.

Let us look at what happens when we fail to apply the principle of forgiveness in our lives. The Bible says, "If you forgive anyone his sins, they are forgiven; if you do not forgive them, they are not forgiven" (John 20: 23). Jesus says, "I tell you the truth, whatever you bind on earth will be bound in heaven, and whatever you loose on earth will be loosed in heaven" (Matthew 18: 18). I understand these scriptures to mean a few things. We have the choice to forgive or not to forgive, whatever the offense. Forgiving someone can manifest freedom for not only the offender, but also the offended. You may say, "I am not interested in 'freeing' that person who has wronged me." That may be so, but if you don't forgive, the converse is also true. If you continue to bind up someone for their wrong doings, you too will be bound up by your own unforgiveness.

You see, when you hold a grudge against someone, you are still in bondage to that person. You are still looking for something from that person, whether it is getting an apology, having the wrong righted, finding revenge, seeing them suffer or whatever. They may never give you what you are looking for. Nevertheless, you remain in *their control* because *you won't let them go*. If you forgive, that means you let the situation and the person go. You are no longer looking for anything from them, so they can't hurt you anymore. Your sense of happiness and peace is no longer dependent on what they do or don't do for or to you. Additionally, you can and should release them into God's hands, for then He is free to deal with them as He sees fit. The Lord's mercies endure, not just for us, but for all who call upon Him. Remember, it is easy to feel love toward those who treat you well. The very nature of forgiveness, though, is that it is for those who have committed an offense, not for those who have been kind to you.

I have been a practicing physical therapist for thirteen years. In that time, I have treated people with both injuries to their bodies as well as disease processes. Though I have done no formal scientific research in this area, I have come to some personal conclusions based on my observations and experiences in professional practice. This is certainly not true *in all cases*, but many patients that I have seen with certain types of degenerative diseases often struggle with issues of unforgiveness and bitterness. I have seen many patients with cancers, arthritic conditions, and auto-immune diseases living with unresolved anger and resentment. I must repeat that *not everyone who has these health issues is necessarily harboring unforgiveness or the like in his heart.* There can be many triggers to sickness, such as trauma as well as genetic and environmental factors. But lifestyle can also play a major role in a person's health, and holding on to unforgiveness is a lifestyle choice. I do believe that for some, even many, holding onto grudges or anger can actually turn the body against itself. In short, your emotional and spiritual health can greatly affect your physical health.

I remember a man who came to see me for relief of an arthritic condition. As we worked together, I listened to him speak. He displayed a critical, negative, and bitter attitude. In a word, he was a grouch. I remember thinking to myself that his body had begun to reflect what was in his heart. They were both hard, rigid, and painful. The Bible says in Proverbs 27: 19, "As water reflects a face, so a man's heart reflects the man." Even though he was a difficult personality to work with, I truly felt sorry for him. He gave off nastiness because that is what was in his heart. That must be a difficult condition to perpetually live in.

I write this section on forgiveness because it is so very important. There is so much that we can learn from this and that we can use to improve the present and future conditions of our lives. If there is someone in your life that you need to be reconciled with, seek God and do your part to make peace. Remember, there are no second chances after someone dies. I have seen many people torn up inside because they never reconciled with or heard what they felt they needed to hear from a loved one before that person died. Conversely, I have seen lives that were once filled with pain because of abuse or neglect become completely restored because some form of forgiveness had transpired. Someone has to rise up and break the harsh wall of bitterness with love, as Jesus so often did.

A few weeks before Jeanne died, we had a heart-to-heart talk. It was a talk that I will never forget for as long as I live. During our conversation, she told me that she was going to die soon. She also told me what she thought of me and how she felt, having had me for her sister. I got to tell her how I felt as well. The exchanges were all loving and positive. It's not that we had never had a disagreement over 34 years of being sisters, but all of our differences just melted away in that moment. We knew we loved each other above all and had each forgiven each other for whatever might have gone wrong in the past. It just didn't matter anymore. It was wonderful! I feel very fortunate to have had that time with my sister. With my brother Vinnie, we had no warning of his impending death. But still, I have such peace remembering the very last words that we spoke to each other. We were talking on the phone and our last words to each other were "I love you." I consider these two scenarios as gifts from God, and I am grateful that one of the last memories I have of my brother and sister are loving and peaceful. It has helped me during some of the more intense periods of grief. I don't have to look back at my last moments with them with regret. I pray you will learn from this.

Please understand that this chapter is not meant to be a catalyst for guilt. The Bible says in Romans 3: 23, "... all fall short of the glory of God...." None of us are perfect. My last moments with my sister and brother could have just as easily been negative rather than positive. We are not always everything we should be. Maybe you are wishing you could have been reconciled to your deceased loved one, but now it is too late. Believe it or not, you can still do something about it. If you need to forgive someone who has already died, you can still do that, even now. It will really free you and bring you peace. Conversely, if you find yourself in a place where you may be feeling guilty for things done or not done, said or not said, go to God and ask for forgiveness.

For a time, I wrestled with feelings of guilt about whether or not I could have done something to save my brother. I was barraged with thoughts like, "If only you had... done more... said something different... let him know in a deeper way how much you cared... Vinnie would still be here." I thought the same of other family members. I was even angry with Vinnie for not doing more to help himself. I remember screaming at Vinnie in my kitchen shortly after he passed away, furious that he had left us, wondering if he was happy now for what he had done to us. Logically, I realized that those were wrong thoughts, aimed at pulling me and others down into a pit of condemnation. But when we are in pain, our thoughts are not always logical. Eventually, after much struggle, I was able to let those thoughts go. Emotionally though, it was still very difficult to recognize that there was nothing else that I could have done for my brother. Nevertheless, I knew I *had* done my very best. We had *all* done our best; so did Vinnie.

A few days after this revelation, I went to the cemetery, where Vinnie's and Jeanne's graves lie along side each other. It is the only place left on earth where I can feel *physically* close to my brother and sister. I realize that they are not actually at the cemetery, but it is a physical place for me to go and pay respects to their memory. And though it may sound funny, I do my best talking to them there. I fell to my knees at his grave and cried like a baby, telling Vinnie that I understood. I told him that I had forgiven him for dying and that I could let him go now, because I knew he was at peace, and that was where he needed to be. I asked him to forgive me if there was anything I could have done to make a better difference in his life. Then I told Vinnie what I told him to say to Jeanne when he was grieving for her. I said, "So long Vin, I'll see you soon".

I believe that we need to use our experiences to make the necessary changes in our lives, to improve both our present and our future. Don't let yourself get stuck in the pain of the past. It's okay to look back for a time, if you will learn from your past, but always keep your eyes fixed on what lies ahead. Try not to go to bed angry or leave the house being mad at your loved ones. Don't hang up the phone on someone without leaving them with a kind, loving word. Tell someone special that you love them. These suggestions can be challenging at times and may not always seem to be practical. But even when dealing with the most difficult of personalities, we must put aside our pride and demonstrate some form of love. I hope you will do your part, no matter what anyone else does or gives back to you. You will help to build a brighter future for yourself.

## Chapter Five

# Healing

This is a difficult chapter to write because I find myself seeking my own healing even at this time. Jeanne died less than two years ago, and Vinnie died just over one year ago. While I have experienced a tremendous amount of healing in my heart to date, I know that there is much more to come. I am writing this at the beginning of the holiday season for 1998. I feel that I am miles ahead of where I was this time last year. But still, I find myself crying in the shopping malls when I hear Christmas carols over the intercom system or just crying because thoughts of my brother and sister come into my head.

I share these and other similar experiences with you because I want you to know that I either was or am where you may be, emotionally speaking. But this is just the tip of the iceberg. This chapter will show you what I have done to experience real healing for my broken heart thus far. The Bible says, "Praise be to the God and Father of our Lord Jesus Christ, the Father of compassion and the God of all comfort, who comforts us in all our troubles, so that we can comfort those in any trouble with the comfort we ourselves have received from God. For just as the sufferings of Christ flow over into our lives, so also through Christ our comfort overflows" (2 Corinthians 1; 3 - 5). I pray that this will bless you.

---

## I believe that in order for you to *heal from* your pain, you must *deal with* your pain.

---

I believe that in order for you to *heal from* your pain, you must *deal with* your pain. I say this because pain is really just a symptom of deeper issues. Let me illustrate by using our human bodies as an example. If you begin to feel pain in your tooth, the dentist does not just give you a pain killer and send you on your way. He investigates to find the cause of the pain. It might be a cavity, an exposed nerve, an abscess, or something else. The dentist cannot effectively treat your toothache unless he first determines the cause of the pain.

It is the same with emotional pain. It is just a symptom of deeper issues that we are struggling with. After the loss of a loved one, most people might think that it is evident why a person is in pain—they are grieving their loss. When someone closely related to you dies, you will likely feel some sense of pain, right? Where is the great revelation here? I can agree with this idea, but I have taken it a step further by going beyond the obvious. It is important to examine what is *in* the pain that you are feeling, in order to work through it. Some people do this by way of professional counseling, talking with a trusted confidante, going to the Lord in prayer, or some combination thereof. Whatever way you choose, I believe that this step is critical to receiving God's healing for your broken heart.

Let's take a look at what I mean. Suppose you have just lost your spouse. At the root of the pain you are feeling may be underlying feelings such as sadness, fear, or anger, to name a few. For example, the most obvious reason to feel sadness would be that your spouse is no longer with you. He or she is not here anymore to love you or to receive your love. But there may be *sadness* because of certain dreams or plans that you had with your spouse that will never come to fruition. Perhaps you were planning to have children together. Maybe you already have children or even grandchildren, and there is sadness at the thought that your spouse will not see the children grow up. You may be in *fear* about facing your future without your spouse or about taking on the tasks that your spouse always did. Many people struggle with fears of how they will meet their financial responsibilities after their mate has passed. You may feel *angry* when you think about why this had to happen to you and your spouse. Perhaps she was young and you think it was unfair that her life was taken seemingly prematurely. Perhaps she suffered and you are angry about that.

There are a myriad of possible circumstances and feelings to match those circumstances. The bottom line is, whatever the situation and whatever the accompanying emotions, I believe that you must allow these emotions to "come up" from within you so you can properly deal with them and be healed. If we don't know what is directing our emotional state, we cannot effectively deal with or treat it, just as in the example of the dentist. Once you identify what it is that you are feeling, feel it and let it come up so that you can begin to get through it. Denying your feelings in the name of being "strong" will never help you move through them. Remember, "ya gotta deal to heal." This may sound ironic, but it is not an easy thing to really *feel* what you are feeling. It can really hurt. Many people "stuff" their feelings, or never let them come up to feel them, because they anticipate them to be too painful to experience. That may be so for a time. I know that after Vinnie died, there were places I could not go emotionally because I knew I was unable to cope with them. The feelings were so intense that I could not process them all at the same time. I felt like I would have died.

Eventually though, gradually and over time, *all* of your feelings should be dealt with constructively or you will not experience full healing. You will need help doing this. God *wants* to help you with this. Taking your pain and concerns to the Lord in prayer is one of the best ways I know of to experience true and lasting healing. Having wise and loving people in your life that you can confide in can be a truly blessed resource for something like this. They are like gifts from God. If you need professional help, seek out a qualified Christian counselor.

Some people get stuck in certain places that they cannot or do not want to come out of. For example, when mourning the loss of a loved one, a person may become depressed or angry. While this can be very normal, *staying* in a state of depression or anger is not. This is very unhealthy and is often mistaken for grieving. Grief is a God-given process which allows human beings the ability to work through and release intense pain. It is a dynamic process which eventually permits the grieving party to move forward with his life. *Remaining depressed and angry will never release pain, it will only increase pain.* It will keep you stuck in that same place for as long as you allow it. Dealing with pain does not mean that you stay *in* it either. However, going through your grief process at a pace that you can handle is a healthy and productive way to release the pain and puts you in a position for true healing to occur.

After a feeling begins to well up in me, I go to the Lord with it in prayer. Sometimes I confide in someone who I know will give me sound counsel. I also look to see what God says in His Word about my situation and then begin to meditate on that Word. In any case, I always get the guidance and comfort I need to really deal with the issue head on. As I work with the Lord on the issue, I gradually begin to feel a release from that particular source of pain. (It does not always happen overnight though.)

For example, among the many intense feelings that were aroused in me after losing my two siblings was a feeling of fear. Losing Jeanne was one thing. I could rationalize to myself that other people in the world have had close relatives who got sick and died. This time, it happened in my family. But I figured that our family had been dealt our share of heartache and that we were now precluded from further tragedy. So when Vinnie, a young, healthy marathon runner, died, just four and a half months later, it blew my mind. My entire foundation was rocked, and I had no sense of security or safety for my future or the future of my loved ones. I simply could not understand how a thing like this could happen. How could I have lost half of my siblings (they being 36 years young) in just under five months? I was shaken at my core. I remember feeling so frightened that I could not help thinking, "What's next? Who's next?"

It is precisely these thoughts and feelings that I took to the Lord. It was then, when I chose to deal with my feelings, that I learned to trust God. Rather than pretend that I wasn't having these feelings, I squarely faced them and decided to give God a crack at them. I couldn't seem to get rid of them on my own, and hanging on to them was only hurting me. So, in my prayer time, I told God what was troubling me. I told Him that I felt frightened. I was frightened for my safety, well-being, and future, and that of my family. I told God that I did not want to struggle with this anymore but that I did not know how to over-come this particular problem. God knew exactly what my problem was and exactly what I needed, even before I spoke those words to Him. After all, He's God! But I had to choose to bring it to Him before He could help me. It was an act of submission and trust. I chose to trust in a power greater than myself—Almighty God! God will not violate our wills. We can choose to hang on to our fears, pain, anger, and whatever other problems that may be binding us up; or we can choose to give them to the Lord. As a child will give the broken pieces of his toy to his father to fix, let God have the broken pieces of your life. He will take joy in the mending.

As I submitted to the Lord, it was then that the Holy Spirit put me in remembrance of the scripture in 2 Timothy 1: 7, which says, "For God did not give us a spirit of fear, but a spirit of power, of love and of a sound mind." During the times that I experience intense fear, I hang on to this scripture as if it is the very air that I breathe because it is what I need to get me through. When my mind wants to dwell on negative, fearful thoughts, I begin to refocus on what the Word of God says about those thoughts. As I meditate on God's perspective, I allow His Holy Spirit to minister peace, comfort, and consolation to my heart. As a result, over time, God is healing me of these painful feelings.

Jesus spoke to His disciples about the Holy Spirit referring to him as *the Counselor*: "Unless I go away, the Counselor will not come to you; but if I go, I will send him to you... But when he, the Spirit of truth, comes, he will guide you into all truth. He will not speak on his own; he will speak only what he hears, and he will tell you what is yet to come. He will bring glory to me by taking from what is mine and making it known to you" (John 16: 7, 13, 14). The Holy Spirit can minister the peace and comfort of God to our hearts, minds, emotions, and whatever else might need healing. He ministers to us not on His own behalf, but straight from the throne of God. It is the best medicine I know of.

As I mentioned before, this healing does not necessarily come all at once and overnight. It can take time, and sometimes I find myself dealing with the same feelings over and over again. I can remember right after Vinnie died, I would wake up in the middle of the night, sweating and panting, wondering if my family was alive. First, I would check my husband, to see if he was still breathing. I would watch the rise and fall of his chest. If it was too subtle to notice, I would wait until I saw him make some voluntary movement with his body to indicate life. Then, when I was satisfied, I would get up and hurriedly check my two beautiful children—desperate to feel that tiny flow of air on my finger that I held just below their nostrils. You see, my brother had passed away in his sleep, and evidently, subconsciously, I was afraid that my husband and children might not wake up once they went to sleep. Fear is a terrible thing!

Sometimes I can still jolt out of a sound sleep with those same tormenting, fearful thoughts, but I try to take a different approach. Rather than feed into the fear, I get control over it with God's Word. I think on a peaceful thought of God's protection for my family and me. For example, Psalm 91 and verse 5 says, "You will not fear the terror of night, nor the arrow that flies by day." I begin to meditate on this verse, and then others come to mind. If I can't think of any on my own, I open up my bible and begin reading until I find scripture to meet my need at that moment. I have frequently referred to Psalm 4: 8, which says, "I will lie down and sleep in peace, for you alone, O Lord, make me dwell in safety." Sometimes I just insert the names of my family members into this verse where appropriate and claim this promise of God for them and for myself. I say a prayer and leave them in God's loving hands. I may still get up to check on the children, as most mothers do, but it is not with a feeling of impending doom. I pray over them, kiss them, trust them to God, and try to leave all fearful thoughts behind because I am instead choosing to trust God and the promises of His Word. Incidentally, reading from the book of Psalms before bed is a great way to end your day and have peaceful sleep.

This past weekend, I went to a family wedding. It was a very festive and joyful time of celebration for the families at this occasion. It was, however, the first time I had been at a wedding or any such affair since my sister and brother passed away. As happy as I was for my cousin (the groom) and his new bride, I found my heart breaking inside of me as I thought of my missing siblings. The last wedding that my family and I were all together for was my brother Vinnie's. What a great time we had! We filled up an entire table because we were so many. Now, the places where Jeanne and Vinnie would have been sitting, with their partners, were taken by other well-wishers to the bride and groom. When I see my other brother and sister and myself together, like at this wedding, I also see how few we really are now. I cannot help but feel a void; it is like a piece of my heart has been torn out. My body was at the wedding, but my heart and mind were busy grieving: feeling and thinking about my loss. No matter how hard I tried to engage in the celebration, I simply could not "be there." All I could do was struggle to fight back the tears.

It took me another day or so to get past this terrible sadness that came over me. It wasn't easy, but I did. Here's what happened. The day after the wedding, I was still overwhelmed with grief. Just like the night before, I tried to be brave for the sake of my family. I didn't want to upset anyone by crying, so I kept trying to push my sadness down. Everytime I wanted to cry, I just swallowed the pain and tried to keep a stiff upper lip. I felt like I was going to burst, and in a way, I did. I felt like the dike that the little Dutch boy had his finger in. I tried to plug up the hole temporarily, but eventually the pressure was too great and the floodgates opened.

My husband could tell that something was wrong, and all he had to do was ask, "What is the matter?" I sat at the kitchen table with my face buried in my hands and sobbed. I told him why I was crying. My husband, desperate to make me feel better, attempted to console me by telling me to stop crying. He didn't want me to feel anymore pain. Maybe he figured that if I just pushed it aside, it would go away. He found out it doesn't work that way.

As my husband stroked my shoulders, he whispered, "It's okay, don't cry, don't cry." I remember my reaction was strong and swift. I yelled out, "No! Let me cry! Just let me cry and feel this! Just let me get it out!" We both allowed me to feel the pain of my loss that morning by having a very good cry. After I shed my last tear, I could take a full, deep breath again. It was very cleansing and provided me with much needed relief. Sometimes you just have to go through it to be able to move past it.

I decided, though, that once I let these feelings come up, I was not going to dwell on negative thoughts. That would be very depressing and counter-productive to healing. I remembered the scripture that says, "Rejoice in the Lord always. I will say it again: Rejoice! Let your gentleness be evident to all. The Lord is near. Do not be anxious about anything, but in everything, by prayer and petition, with thanksgiving, present your requests to God. And the peace of God, which transcends all understanding, will guard your hearts and your minds in Christ Jesus" (Philippians 4: 4 - 7).

After I finished crying, the next thing I did was ask God to take this pain from me. I asked Him to help me to accept that my siblings weren't here anymore. I thanked Him for the family that I did have around me and asked Him to help me refocus my attention to them. Then I asked for His peace. In no time at all, my heart and mind was filled with His peace again.

---

**Feeling the pain and then giving it to God—seeking His word and allowing His Holy Spirit to minister to my needs, has worked very well for me.**

---

Feeling the pain and *then giving it to God*—seeking His Word and allowing His Holy Spirit to minister to my needs—has worked very well for me. I pray that you will try the same wherever you need healing in your life.

Understand that the loss of a loved one can affect many aspects of your life and the life of your family. It can, in essence, change the entire complexion of a family. Holidays are never the same. There are less people present at family gatherings. When we sit down for a family meal, I sometimes still wait for Jeanne and Vinnie to take their seats with the rest of us, only to remember that they cannot. There have been occasions that something exciting has happened and I have wanted to share it with either of the twins. I have actually picked up the phone to call them only to be disappointed at the realization that they would not be on the other end of the line. Sometimes, only certain people will do when you need to talk something over. When those certain people are not there for you anymore, it can feel like you are the loneliest person in the world.

These are the changes that we must slowly but surely assimilate into our lives as we heal. Doing this can be most difficult. When a person dies, we not only mourn the loss of that person but also of how life was *supposed* to be. We mourn the expectations that we had for our lives with that person. I mourn the loss of potential nieces and/or nephews I might have had if Jeanne and Vinnie had lived. Case in point: I was very angry last weekend when I was faced with processing the change of not having my brother and sister present at the wedding. I resented that I had to do it. I wanted them to be there with the rest of us! It just wasn't the same without them. It didn't seem fair!

I am reasonably sure, though, that this process will get easier as I go along. It has already gotten easier over this past year. I believe that part of what is making this transition phase possible for me is my decision to "let go," a little at a time. The healing that I experience is proportional to how much I let go. I have observed other people who experienced significant loss long before I did, and they have not even begun to enter this phase of healing. It may be largely due to their unwillingness to let go.

It is difficult to let go, and you don't have to do it if you don't want to. But you will never really be healed either. The saying "Time heals all wounds" is not really accurate, in my opinion. I believe it is *what you do over time* that will determine whether your wounds get healed. You can stay where you are—it is your choice. Sometimes the pain itself can be in some ways comforting because we can hang on to it when it seems like there is nothing else to hang on to. Letting go of pain can be scary. What is on the other side of that pain? Between the time of letting go and actually feeling some happiness, there is a period of unknown. It is that fear of the unknown that I believe prevents people from stepping out of their pain and into freedom.

But staying with the pain for the rest of your life is very difficult to do also. There is a price to pay. I know because before I made a decision to move in the direction of healing, I hung on to the pain. It brought me security because it was familiar and I could count on it being there *all the time*. But it was taking a toll on my body and my psyche. Those who know me best have characterized me as happy, up-beat, and someone who likes to laugh. That was changing—at least when I was at home. I began to experience chest pains and difficulty breathing. I was either crying from feelings of depression or shouting a lot at my children and husband because of feelings of anger. I was worried about my parents' physical and emotional condition, and I silently lived with the fear that something else was going to happen to somebody else in our family.

It was during a conversation I had with my husband Randy, one night, that I finally realized I needed to make a change. I realized that I needed to let go. It was just over one year that Jeanne had died and a couple of months shy of one year marking Vinnie's passing. We had had a fun day and a lovely evening and decided to retire to our bedroom. As we were lying in bed, my husband reached over to snuggle with me. He leaned over to kiss my cheek and noticed tears streaming down my face. When he asked me what was wrong, all I could say was, "I am just so, so sad." After a few questions, he understood I was referring to the loss of the twins. As usual, he patiently tried to comfort and encourage me. This time, though, he said something that I had never heard him say before.

As he held me, he said, "I just want *us* to be happy again, the way we used to be." Those were sobering words. Evidently, *my* pain had become *his* pain. It was affecting my immediate family, yet I had not been able to see just how much because the pain had begun to blind me. I thought my suffering was self-contained: I was wrong. Now I felt guilty for allowing my grief to pour over into my own immediate family. Randy was certainly not *trying* to make me feel guilty—he was just expressing his sadness at how these tragedies had affected me, our little family, and our lives. I was glad that he felt he could tell me how *he* felt in all this, but now I had something else to deal with. My heart broke yet again because I never wanted this to happen, nor did I want it to continue. This night and Randy's words were a call to change. My husband encouraged me to do something constructive with these feelings that I was having. Ultimately, that conversation was what inspired me to write this book.

---

**I believe that this principle of reframing how you see the circumstances in your life is at the core of your ability to cope and survive crises and tragedy.**

---

Letting go is scary because it means different things to different people. A couple of months after Jeanne died, my brother Vinnie called me to talk about Jeanne again and the pain he was experiencing. I will never forget the question he asked me: "Fran, how did you say 'good-bye' to her? I just can't bring myself to say 'good-bye.'" I replied, "Vinnie, I haven't said 'good-bye' to Jeanne. I couldn't bear it either. I've just said, 'so-long, see you again soon.'" (I felt confident that I would see Jeanne again in heaven.) I just took the same situation that Vinnie was dealing with and framed it differently than he did. What once seemed unbearable suddenly became bearable because I chose to reframe the situation with different thinking. *I believe that this principle of reframing how you see the circumstances in your life is at the core of your ability to cope and survive crises and tragedy.*

But just as Vinnie was having trouble letting go after Jeanne died, I realized that I was experiencing the same trouble letting go after they had *both* died. I suppose I had the internal resources to cope better with the loss of Jeanne simply because it was just that—one loss. With Vinnie's passing right on the heels of Jeanne's and without having the chance to fully grieve for Jeanne, the proverbial final straw was beginning to break my back: two significant losses so close together. Now I was having real trouble processing the whole situation.

Randy told me that I needed to let go. Walking by an old photography studio once, I noticed an inscription that read: "There is no present (gift) like the past." I did not want to let go of that gift. I was so wrapped up in the old world that I did not want to let go of it. I told Randy that I was afraid to let go because I didn't want to ever forget them. It may seem irrational to some, but I was afraid that if I let go, any trace of their existence would just vanish from the face of the earth. I couldn't bear the memory of their lives fading away. I went from having four siblings to two in just four and a half months. I had lost enough; I was not interested in letting go and losing anything else. I was also afraid to let go because I did not know what I would hold on to. What would be there to replace the pain? At least I had pain to hold on to, when everything else in my life and the life of my family seemed so uncertain. The unknown can be so frightening.

In that same conversation with my husband, Randy helped me to reframe my thoughts and fears about letting go of the pain of the loss of the twins. I realized that letting go does not mean forgetting or erasing. It just means *releasing* the hopes, dreams, and expectations that I had for my family and embracing the *truth* of the current reality.

In a poignant sermon, a pastor once pointed out the difference between truth and reality. *Reality* is the current condition of your life. *Truth* is what God says about and wants for your life. Reality is that my sister's and brother's physical lives on this earth have ended. But the truth is that death does not erase a life, but rather, it reinforces it. This book is living proof of such a statement.

*Having the truth is finding a way to go on with my life and make my life really count for something, despite the reality of these devastating and tragic losses.* For me, letting go means that it is okay to have a loving, intimate moment with my husband and not feel guilty. It means enjoying my children's laughter and being able to genuinely laugh with them and then not feeling ashamed of being without pain for that moment. It was here that I began to accept the fact that it was my sister and brother who died... *and I didn't!* I didn't have to stop living just because they did. God has more living for me to do. Letting go has given me permission to live out my life as God intended me to live it. I just took it a step at a time and worked very slowly so that I didn't get ahead of myself.

---

**The truth, though, is that their
death doesn't have to take
your life!**

---

*Remember, letting go does not mean forgetting.* There is an old expression that goes something like this: "A person dies *only* when we forget them." Jeanne and Vinnie are now and always will be an integral part of my life and in my heart and memories. I talk about them all the time and still draw much from their lives by remembering past experiences I had with them. Our loved ones could never be forgotten by us. Your current reality may be that you lost someone in your life that you loved dearly. *The truth, though, is that their death doesn't have to take your life!* All you have to do is have the courage to set down some of your pain, even if it's just for a short while. Then allow yourself to feel something else, something positive, even if it's just for a short while. With practice, you will find yourself feeling the good in life again, and the sharp intensity of the pain will begin to dull.

The process of letting go and healing is allowing me to fulfill the call of God on my life, even though Jeanne's and Vinnie's physical life on earth has come to an end. It is not always easy though. Remember my cousin's wedding earlier in this chapter. I could not find the desire or strength to really celebrate there—it was just too painful. I could not let go. That's okay, though, because the first time experiencing anything like that is always the hardest. As time goes by, believe it or not, it does and I trust will continue to get easier.

As you allow God to heal your heart, if you find that you have an emotional setback, don't get discouraged. Just realize that it is all part of the experience of grief. Take the time you need to properly mourn. Then as you give the pieces of your broken heart to the Lord, watch how He transforms your pain into joy and gladness. Keep pushing forward towards the mark of true healing—with God's grace, you will reach it. Let go of the pain and fill the hollowness in your heart with God.

# Chapter Six

# Fully Alive

Chapter two in this book deals with the subject of "living again." First, I discuss making the decision to live again with spirit and purpose. Second, I explain why it is not just acceptable but our responsibility to God, our loved ones, and ourselves to fully live again. This point bears repeating. Each of us has a divine purpose in life. Not to live out that purpose is an utter shame and a waste of a life; I believe it grieves the Holy Spirit of God. The apostle Paul writes, "I keep asking that the God of our Lord Jesus Christ, the glorious Father, may give you the Spirit of wisdom and revelation, so that you may know him better. I pray also that the eyes of your heart may be enlightened in order that you may know the hope to which he has called you, the riches of his glorious inheritance in the saints, and his incomparably great power for us who believe" (Ephesians 1: 17 - 19). God wants us to be fully alive unto Him!

If you have decided to live again, and I hope you have, you may be wondering *how* to do just that. You may truly desire to pick up the pieces of your life and get on with the business of living but may not know where to start. It is profoundly difficult to move forward with your life when it seems like your world, your life as you once knew it, has just fallen apart. In fact, it may even seem nearly impossible. I remember a day, just weeks after my brother died, when I felt just that.

I was taking my daughter to nursery school. I did not even want to get dressed that day, let alone have to leave the house and converse with people that I would inevitably meet along the way. But grief knows no boundaries. It doesn't give you a reprieve so that you can go on with the duties of your life, sadness-free! Unless you choose to totally check-out of this life, you are faced with carrying on with the normal tasks and responsibilities of your life while trying to cope with the intense burden of your grief. I found this aspect of grief particularly difficult to handle. At times, I even felt resentful. It just seemed that the needs of those who depended on me always came before my need to grieve.

As I brought my daughter into her nursery school, I stared at the long corridor that we had to walk down; it was filled with people. Happy mothers and chipper teachers were talking and laughing. The place was buzzing, and I dreaded being there. I hung my head as I started down the hallway, hoping that no one would notice me or stop me. All around me, chirpy voices were chatting and giggling. Women were talking about carpools and the cupcakes they were bringing in for their child's class party. I thought I would go out of my mind. I couldn't stand it anymore. I wanted to scream, and in my mind I thought, "Stop! Don't you people know what has happened? How can you so callously talk about carpools and cupcakes when my family and I have lost so much?! Don't you understand?"

I dropped off my daughter and ran for the exit door. When I got outside, I took in a deep breath of fresh air, feeling like I had escaped a time warp. I got into my car, eager to get home. But before I could put the key in the ignition, my head dropped to the steering wheel and I just cried. The women at the school had done nothing wrong. They were not being purposely insensitive. They didn't even know what had happened. They were just going about their normal business of living. So what was my problem? It was then that I realized what was happening to me. I was being asked to live in an *externally normal world* when *internally*, my world was *not normal* at all. My world felt like it had fallen apart.

If you are in a state of mourning, especially in the acute phase, it can be a wrenching experience to have to fit into the normal outside world when your personal world is so abnormal. It is very lonely to be outwardly participating in everyday activities with others when these same people don't have a clue as to the degree of inward pain you are in. It is almost like being a third person watching from the outside in.

Additionally, even the simplest of tasks become difficult, and the easiest of jobs can drain your energy. It can be unnerving to watch everyone else scurrying about the business of life, without missing a beat, while you struggle to get dressed and maybe place one important phone call or run one mundane errand. This is because grief is a dynamic process that requires an extraordinary amount of energy. Your body and mind are expending so much energy coping with your situation. For some, energy is being used just to fight to stay alive. However the regular, *normal* responsibilities of your life still demand your attention. Therefore, as you attempt to carry on with the business of living, it can feel quite exhausting. This is why if you know someone who has experienced a loss, it is nice to try to lend a hand where you can. Maybe you can offer to baby-sit or run errands. Your doing laundry or passing the vacuum through their house might be appreciated. If the person won't accept or ask for help, just bring a meal or a bag of essential groceries anyway. Doing these chores may seem insignificant to you and may not cost you much by way of time or effort. But for the person who feels drained or overwhelmed by their circumstances, it can mean so much.

This chapter will help you find ways, both practical and spiritual, to begin living again, even when it seems abnormal to do so. I do not have a set formula for you to follow; everyone's life, circumstances, callings, and conflicts are very different. I do believe, though, that there are some heart attitudes that must be in place in order for you to live wholly. Even if they are not in place in your life now, they can be cultivated with a little effort.

One ingredient to fully living is having a *heart at peace*. You cannot live out your purpose for being on this earth if you do not have inner peace. Having inner peace does not mean that your life runs perfectly and smoothly all the time or that you never make a mistake or never lose your temper. It does not mean that every "i" is dotted and every "t" is crossed. For me, knowing that I am walking in God's perfect will for my life brings me inner peace. I did not say *my walking perfectly* brings me inner peace; in that case, I would never have peace. Rather, walking in His *perfect will* is what brings me peace. That is, doing what I believe the Father wants me to do and walking in a manner worthy and pleasing of Him.

Saint Paul writes, "For this reason, since the day we heard about you, we have not stopped praying for you and asking God to fill you with the knowledge of his will through all spiritual wisdom and understanding. And we pray this in order that you may live a life worthy of the Lord and may please him in every way: bearing fruit in every good work, growing in the knowledge of God, being strengthened with all power according to his glorious might so that you may have great endurance and

patience, and joyfully giving thanks to the Father, who has qualified you to share in the inheritance of the saints in the kingdom
of light" (Colossians 1: 9 - 12). What a beautiful passage of
Scripture that can be applied to our lives today. As we walk in
the knowledge of God's will, we will be strengthened and have
great endurance and patience. This translates into having a
heart at peace.

I also have peace knowing that when I miss the mark and sin,
the finished work of Jesus Christ on Calvary covers my sin and I
am forgiven: "If we confess our sins, he is faithful and just and
will forgive us our sins and purify us from all unrighteousness"
(1 John 1: 9). Peace is knowing that no matter what happens,
God is in control, even when it appears that He has abandoned
you: "Do not be afraid or terrified because of them, for the Lord
your God goes with you; he will never leave you nor forsake you"
(Deuteronomy 31: 6). God does not abandon us; it only looks
like that sometimes. As you trust Him with your life, you will
have peace.

**It is not a question of whether you will have trouble in this life; rather, it is a question of *how* you will cope with it.**

Stress is something that we hear a lot about. Most people
understand that stress can severely adversely affect a person's
health by robbing one's peace. Likewise, many of us have heard
advice to avoid stress at all costs. But if you have endured the
pain of the loss of a loved one, you have stress! There is no
getting around it. Besides, even Jesus did not promise us a life

without stress or problems. But He does promise us a way out. In John 16: 33, Jesus says, "I have told you these things, so that in me you may have peace. In this world you will have trouble. But take heart! I have overcome the world."

It is not a question of whether you will have trouble in this life; rather, it is a question of *how* you will cope with it. We can be encouraged by the words of the prophet Isaiah: "When you pass through the waters, I will be with you; and when you pass through the rivers, they will not sweep over you. When you walk through the fire, you will not be burned; the flames will not set you ablaze" (Isaiah 43: 2). God wants us to have peace even in the middle of the most stressful crisis we can imagine. Managing stress is a way to have a peaceful heart, and the Christian has Jesus to help him.

I remember years ago signing up my mother and myself for a stress reduction class as a birthday present to her. Things didn't work out too well, though, because we ended up more stressed out after going to this stress reduction class. Either the students were not picking up what the instructor was trying to get across, or he was not communicating effectively, or maybe it was a little bit of both, but we were not grasping just how to reduce our stress.

I still laugh when I remember the night when my mother, out of frustration, raised her hand and said to the instructor, "Excuse me, but I have five children. Do you mean to tell me that if I find out that one of them is on drugs, I'm not supposed to get upset or stressed about it?" We all looked at the teacher, eagerly waiting for some life-changing pearl of wisdom to come forth from his mouth. But the instructor just looked at her and very calmly responded by saying something like, "It does not have to stress you out." What I think was missing in the translation was *how* to not allow our circumstances to stress us out. We wanted to know how to get from point A, experiencing a problem or crisis, to point B, having inner peace amidst the problem or crisis. I don't remember that it was ever forthcoming.

Take heart because there is a lot that we can do to get from point A to point B. In the case of losing a loved one, it is a matter of effectively coping with legitimate grief and integrating into your life the changes that naturally come from suffering such a loss. As previously mentioned, this takes time and can occur through many avenues such as prayer, reading the Word of God, seeking help through family and friends or through a trained professional, to name a few.

After Jeanne and Vinnie died, my family and I spoke daily. We regularly discussed our feelings and difficulties, which I found very helpful in working through the grief. If we lived too far to pay a visit, we talked on the phone. We all "checked-up" on each other. At first we tried to be subtle, but we came to realize that each of us was checking up on the other without wanting the other to know. Finally, it became a joke when we would call and plainly admit, "I'm calling to check up on you, I'm worried. Tell me how you *really* are." In the early days following our losses, if one of us was having a particularly hard time of it, we all seemed to rally around our struggling family member until they got through it. God used all of us to bless each other.

Keeping a journal of your thoughts and feelings as well as reading good books on the subject can also be helpful. If good coping mechanisms are not in operation after a traumatic loss, a person's stress level can become overwhelming. Effectively handling *the stress* of a significant loss in your life can bring you such peace, even in the midst of a storm.

Here are some practical ways you can effectively manage the stress in your life so that you can have a heart of peace. The Bible says in Proverbs 14: 30, "A heart at peace gives life to the body, but envy rots the bones." I see this scripture as a practical application to the benefits of having a peaceful heart. It gives life to the body! We are talking about being fully alive! The most obvious ways to reduce your stress and bring peace to yourself are to eat a healthy and properly balanced diet and to exercise your body. I learned of an acronym a few years ago that I think is applicable in this circumstance. It is G.I.G.O. It stands for, Garbage In Garbage Out. In this application it means that what we put into our bodies and do for our bodies is ultimately what our bodies will give back to us. If you are looking to feel well, both physically and mentally, if you are looking for strength and stamina, you must purpose to fuel your body with the proper foods and eliminate those that would drain your energy. Remember that processing grief requires a lot of energy.

I know that during the 1998 holiday season, I was feeling like my "get up and go" had "gotten up and went." Part of it may have been emotional, but I was not helping matters by indulging in lots of fattening Christmas treats. I usually do that during the holidays. I also did not find time during the busy season to exercise like I normally do. Now that I have returned to normal healthy eating and regular exercise, I have much more energy, patience, and stamina, which ultimately translates into a form of peace. You may require the assistance of a physician or other health professional to obtain a healthy and safe diet and exercise program for you. The point is, be good to yourself! If you take proper care of yourself, you will be better able to cope with your problems. You too will have more energy and stamina to do what you need to do in your circumstances.

Another practical way to give peace to your body is to give it proper rest. God placed within us an immune system which is meant to fight off sickness and disease. Some of the ways to boost our immune system to do its job are eating right, exercising, and getting enough rest. In Matthew 11: 28, Jesus says to His followers, "Come to me, all you who are weary and burdened, and I will give you rest." Jesus knows that the pressures of life can wear us down if we allow them to, but He tells us to come to Him and He will give us rest. We need rest for our souls *and* our bodies.

Additionally, spending time doing some deep-breathing exercises, even five minutes a day, can really help reduce stress. Deep breathing provides your blood with a greater supply of oxygen, which brings healing to your bodily tissues. It also allows for better relaxation of your muscles, which can contribute to an overall feeling of wellness. Taking care of your physical body may not take away the pain of your loss, but it can increase your ability to cope well and effectively manage your stress.

---

**We will find inner peace when we rest in God's Word because it changes us.**

---

Now let's get back to a more spiritual plane. Besides nurturing your body, you must nurture your spirit and soul. Human beings are comprised of three entities: body, soul, and spirit. The *body* we are all familiar with. It is the component of our being that most people pay the most attention to. It is the flesh that houses our soul and spirit. The *soul* is made up of the mind, the will, and the emotions. It is the part of our being that makes us "tick." It is where we think, purpose, and feel. The *spirit* is that part of us in which God resides and speaks to us (if we are alive unto Him). It is the window of our soul which can connect us to

God. All three components need to be nurtured, not just our body.

Nurturing our soul and spirit is not limited to but should include reading and meditating upon the Word of God. We will find inner peace when we rest in God's Word because it changes us. Just like olives need to soak in water to eliminate their bitterness, we need to soak ourselves in the Scriptures so that the "bitter" parts of us can be pushed out and the Word of God can take its full dimensions in us.

Nurturing our soul and spirit should include time spent alone with the Lord in prayer, praising Him, or just in quiet reflection. For you, it may also mean listening to peaceful music, walking alone on the beach, taking a nature hike, or biking along your favorite path. Whatever you choose, the end should result in a sense of edification. You should feel better and more peaceful inside for having done it.

Nurturing does not just mean providing proper nutrition and exercise, but it also means providing protection. Just as you would naturally shield your body from an unwanted attack, you must shield your soul and spirit from an attack if you want to live peacefully. There are some stresses that we cannot avoid in life; others, we can. For example, you may have lost your home in a hurricane. Short of praying and boarding up your house, there is nothing you can do to prevent this tragedy. You did not seek it; rather it found you. But it is the stresses that we *do* have control over that I wish to focus on in this section.

While we do not have control over *everything* that happens to us, I believe that we do have control over *much* of what happens to us. I believe we are to exercise the wisdom of God in all aspects of our life, especially when it comes to protecting our physical, mental, emotional, and spiritual health. The Bible says, "But whoever listens to me (Wisdom) will live in safety and be at ease, without fear of harm" (Proverbs 1: 33). It goes on: "Then you will understand what is right and just and fair - every good path. For wisdom will enter your heart, and knowledge will be pleasant to your soul. Discretion will protect you, and under-standing will guard you" (Proverbs 2: 9 - 11). Do you notice the protective language that God uses here. God does not wish to bring us harm, but rather peace and safety.

If you are in a situation that is tearing down your soul and draining the life from your spirit, I believe that you ought to prayerfully consider how to better manage it. Remember, God wants good things for your life, not bad. The Lord tells us in Hosea 4: 6, "my people are destroyed from lack of knowl-edge...." There may be certain situations or people that you have unwittingly allowed to rob your peace. You may need to relate differently to them or avoid them all together. Whatever the case, seek God's advice as to how you can best protect your soul and spirit so that they can thrive: "May the God of peace... equip you with everything good for doing his will, and may he work in us what is pleasing to him, through Jesus Christ, to whom be glory forever and ever. Amen" (Hebrews 13: 20, 21).

Another component of being fully alive for God is having a *heart of thanksgiving*. You may be thinking, "How can I be thankful after just losing my loved one. I am distraught and grieved, not thankful." If this or anything like this is your thought, you are not alone. I had the same thought after losing my sister Jeanne and brother Vinnie. I remember it being hard going to church on Sunday mornings, especially during the praise and worship time in the service. I wanted to sing my praises to God but felt so weighed down with overwhelming sadness for my loss that sometimes I just couldn't. Other times, I just mouthed the words to the songs, figuring that maybe sooner or later my heart would catch up with my mouth. Actually, that was good figuring on my part because, eventually, it did. The Bible tells us in 1 Thessalonians 5:18, "give thanks in all circumstances, for this is God's will for you in Christ Jesus." It does not say to give thanks *for* all circumstances, but to give thanks *in* all circumstances.

In the book of Acts, Chapter 16, the Bible tells of Paul's and Silas' imprisonment and says that they praised God. I do not believe that they were praising God *for* their situation, rather they were praising God *in* their situation. As they praised God, an earthquake occurred, their shackles fell from their bodies, and the prison doors blew open. They were supernaturally freed by Almighty God. The same can happen with us. You may not be in a physical prison, but maybe you feel you are in an emotional prison. Begin to give thanks to God and worship Him for who He is and what He can do for you. All the shackles that are around your body and soul will start falling one after the other till you are completely free from the weight of your burden.

I remember going to church one Sunday morning and having a breakthrough with the idea of having a thankful heart, in all situations. I walked into the sanctuary to find my seat. It was still hard for me to come to church, but this Sunday, I was determined to really participate and receive from God. The musicians began to play their instruments, the choir began to sing, and the praise and worship leader began to stir the people to worship the Lord. The music was awesome, and my heart began to flood with joy as my spirit praised my God. It felt so good to have some relief from sorrow. Then, without warning, an inaudible voice began to speak to me: "How can you praise God—your brother and sister are dead! There is nothing to be happy about in this situation, and if you do feel happy, you should be ashamed of yourself." My once raised hands sank to my sides.

The joy that flooded my heart minutes ago was sucked out by what seemed like a mighty vacuum. It was over. I remember thinking to myself, "What just happened? What do I do now?"

Just then, it was like a game of chess began to take place in my head. One thought came to me: "If I begin to praise God and allow myself to feel the joy of the Lord, won't that be disrespecting Jeanne and Vinnie?" The counterthought was, "They would want me to move on." The next thought that came was, "What do you have to be thankful for?" And that is where the chess game turned in favor of praising God. The Holy Spirit spoke strong and loud. My counterthought came: "I have *so much* to be thankful for!" I began to think about my husband and children. I began to think about my parents and still living brother and sister. I was reminded of how blessed we were to have each other and our very supportive extended family and friends. I was praising God for being in this church where I could worship Him in spirit and in truth. And when I thought about Vinnie and Jeanne, I could only imagine, with some envy, how glorious it must be for them to be worshipping God at His throne in heaven. If worshipping in this church could be such an awesome time, what must it be like to worship in the direct presence of Almighty God? At that, I looked up to the cross in the center of the altar and said to myself, "Vinnie, Jeanne, you are in a much better place than I. I'll not hold back, but join my praises with yours, to God."

The shackles trying to encase my soul fell off. The doors to the prison that was holding my spirit captive from praising and worshipping God blew open. I realized that I did not have to focus on the losses in order to legitimately grieve for my brother and sister. I also made a conscious decision not to focus on what was taken from me but rather on what I still had—and I had a lot! It does not take a rocket scientist to know that negative thoughts lead to negative feelings. *Prolonged negativity will adversely affect your body, soul, and spirit. Conversely, positive, thankful thoughts lead to positive, thankful feelings and can only foster a state of happiness, peace, and well-being in any person.*

Thanking God will be difficult if you are blaming God for your circumstances. It is easy to blame God for the bad things that happen to us. When we don't have the answers to our questions, we often lay the cause for our problems at God's feet. If you find yourself blaming God, let me caution you here. Blame can lead to bitterness, and bitterness can ruin your life. It is true that God *allows* certain things to happen, even bad things. You don't have to look far to see pain and suffering in this world. But the root cause of these bad things happening is not God. God is love. He is a healer, a protector, a provider. God is life! His Word tells us this throughout the Bible.

Where the evil of this world stems from is the subject for an entire book, too lengthy for any meaningful discussion here. However, I cannot keep from briefly mentioning that we have an adversary: the devil. He is the enemy of our souls. The Bible says in I Peter 5: 8, "Be self-controlled and alert. Your enemy the devil prowls around like a roaring lion looking for someone to devour." Satan is a real being and is ultimately responsible for the pain and suffering in this world, *not God.* Jesus said, "The thief comes only to steal and kill and destroy; I have come that they may have life, and have it to the full" (John 10: 10).

Why God allows bad things to happen is something that I cannot always answer. Given a particular circumstance, I might be able to offer an idea or two as to why that situation happened. But I cannot say that I always know for sure why certain things happen. I do know one thing though. God is in control, and His plans and purposes will prevail: "And we know that in all things God works for the good of those who love him, who have been called according to his purpose" (Romans 8: 28). We do not understand the mind of God, but if we trust Him, He will give us peace in all circumstances. The Bible says, "The Lord works out everything for his own ends..." (Proverbs 16: 4). He can take even the tragedies of this world and turn them for good: "...But we also rejoice in our sufferings, because we know that suffering produces perseverance; perseverance, character; and character, hope. And hope does not disappoint us..." (Romans 5: 3 - 5).

Let me go a step further. If you are having difficulty grasping any sense of joy, peace, or thanksgiving, you may have to begin to *act* the way you want to *feel*. As I mentioned before, right after losing my sister and brother, I would go to church and, merely as an act of obedience, struggle to raise my hands and sing praises to God. My arms felt like heavy weights. But eventually, over time, my arms got lighter and so did my soul and spirit. I made a decision, though, to give God something to work with. Give Him something. If you can't reach out your hand to Him, give Him your finger. You can even give Him your tears. He will meet you where you are and give back to you so much more than you would have ever imagined: "He gives strength to the weary and increases the power of the weak. Even youths grow tired and weary, and young men stumble and fall; but those who hope in the Lord will renew their strength. They will soar on wings like eagles; they will run and not grow weary, they will walk and not be faint" (Isaiah 40: 39 - 31). It took time, but my strength was renewed like the eagle's, and now when I praise the Lord, I truly feel joyful.

If you are feeling lonely and empty, consider getting involved in activities that help others. By coming out of yourself and your pain and refocusing on the needs of others, you will inadvertently experience a sense of fulfillment and happiness that you

might not otherwise experience. Sometimes you must put yourself in a position of extending love to others in order to receive
the love that you want. Giving out of your own need is a very
powerful thing.

Consider the widow in the 21st chapter of Luke's gospel.
Though she only put two very small copper coins in the temple
treasury, she gave more than the rich people because she gave
out of her poverty. She gave *all* that she had. For example,
maybe your child is deceased and you are missing him very
much. You might want to consider spending time and minister-
ing to a child without a mom or a dad. *You* will probably be
more blessed by your attempts to help than the child you are
helping. Only God knows how much I miss my sister Jeanne and
the very motherly, nurturing, protective ways that she had about
her. Ironically, as I have reached out to other women who were
in need of these same attributes, He has given them to me as
"sisters." I have an especially deep sadness at the loss of my
brother because we shared a very special bond in the things of
God. He was my natural brother, but also my "brother in the
Lord." Likewise, as I have found myself reaching out to others,
God has indeed given me very special "brothers in the Lord."

Finally, having a thankful heart puts you in remembrance of
all the blessings that you do have. When you spend time thinking about the good things in your life, you are less focused on
the sad things in your life. Even if you engage in an attitude of
thankfulness for just a few moments a day, then it is a few
minutes less in your day that you are focused on negative
things. Eventually, your positive, thankful thinking should
increase and your negative thinking decrease.

Every morning before I start my day and every night before I
end my day, I try to consider what I have to be thankful for and
begin to praise God. This does not negate the pain and strug-

gles that I contend with, but it keeps things in perspective for me. In between the thanking, I petition God for help where I need Him. Similarly, while I pray to God for strength and comfort to help me deal with the loss of my siblings, I am also thankful to God for the blessing of having had Jeanne and Vinnie in my life for 34 years. I would have liked more time with them, but I am grateful for the time I did have with them and for the impact that they had on my life. *It is so very important to live a balance of seeing both the happy and sad realities of life.*

**We can allow ourselves to be consumed with thoughts of depression and self-pity, or we can choose to do our part in building ourselves up to deal with whatever we are facing in our lives.**

Managing stress, nurturing and protecting our soul and spirit, and being thankful are ways to help us cope with grief and other stresses. They are a means to help get us through and give us victory over our circumstances, no matter how difficult they may be. I believe it is a matter of mentally realizing that we have a choice of how we will respond to our loss and subsequent situation. We can allow ourselves to be consumed with thoughts of depression and self-pity, or we can choose to do our part in building ourselves up to deal with whatever we are facing in our lives. Either way, we are making a choice. I find it very empowering to know that I really do have choices and that life doesn't just happen to me. I can indeed affect the quality of my life by my attitudes, thoughts, and choices. You can too!

I end this chapter with an exhortation that the apostle Paul wrote to the Philippians. I hope it will encourage you towards a peaceful heart and a thankful heart so that you may be fully alive for God. "Rejoice in the Lord always. I will say it again: Rejoice! Let your gentleness be evident to all. The Lord is near. Do not be anxious about anything, but in everything, by prayer and petition, with thanksgiving, present your requests to God. And the peace of God, which transcends all understanding, will guard your hearts and your minds in Christ Jesus. Finally, brothers, whatever is true, whatever is noble, whatever is right, whatever is pure, whatever is lovely, whatever is admirable—if anything is excellent or praiseworthy—think about such things. Whatever you have learned or received or heard from me, or seen in me—put into practice. And the God of peace will be with you" (Philippians 4: 4 - 9).

*Chapter Seven*

# Remembering a Life

As I mentioned in the love chapter, funerals are, among other things, occasions for people to remember the life that their deceased loved one lived. During these times of reflection, I find that very interesting and enlightening experiences and lessons are retrieved by remembering a life, even when that life, when measured by the world's standards, might have seemed average and ordinary. I notice that people often remember the smallest of details when sharing anecdotes involving their passed on family member or friend. These observations prove something to me. They prove that, even if you are not rich or famous, and even if you have never achieved "huge successes" in your life, your life really does have an impact on this world. That is, we are all making memories everyday (for better or for worse), and these memories make a difference in the lives of those we know as well as in the lives of some that we don't know. Simply put, our actions often touch more people than we realize and in ways that we may not realize.

This point is very well illustrated by examining Frank Capra's movie "It's A Wonderful Life." The main character, George Bailey, thinks of his life as a failure because he never really got his day in the sun. Everyone else around him seemed to be rising to their potential and "succeeding," but not him. This created a sense of frustration and despair in George. Only at the end of the movie does his guardian angel, Clarence, show George how his actions significantly affected the lives of those around him.

---

**Simply put, our actions often touch more people than we realize and in ways that we may not realize.**

---

For example, George's brother Harry, a navy flyer in the war, could not have saved an entire transport of men if George had not saved his brother from drowning when they were children. Harry was named a hero for his acts of bravery in the war, and rightly so. But they would never have been a reality if George had not done his part some 15 or 20 years prior. There were several other examples of this cause and effect relationship between George Bailey's life and the lives of many others, both known and unknown to him. I will not mention them all, as I think the point is well-made. Likewise, your life, ordinary though it may seem, can and does impact many people and things.

This brings me to my next point. Make your life count—for good! Do something with your life that will bring good to others and make this world a better place in which to live. The Bible instructs us in Proverbs 10: 7, "The memory of the righteous will be a blessing, but the name of the wicked will rot." Evidently we will be remembered; it's a matter of *how* we will be remembered. I believe that we should behave in such a manner as we would like to be remembered (hopefully positively). Most people wish to be remembered or spoken of with fondness; however, not everyone with this desire conducts themselves in a manner deserving of it. If your goal is to be remembered positively, your actions should be reflective of this goal.

The best way to be beloved by many is to come out of yourself and give of yourself. Be the first to reach out and give to someone instead of looking for someone to give to you. Live a life of service. Jesus came as a servant. After washing His disciples' feet, Jesus said to them, "Now that I, your Lord and Teacher, have washed your feet, you also should wash one another's feet. I have set you an example that you should do as I have done for you" (Luke 13: 14, 15). The Bible also says, "It is more blessed to give than to receive" (Acts 20: 35). There are so many unmet needs out there. Everywhere your feet walk—in your community, on your street, and I'm sure even in your own family—there are big and small needs. Don't wait for someone else to fill them. You will be more blessed in your doing and giving than the recipients of your efforts.

I must caution you though. True, sincere, pure giving does not seek an audience. We must give of ourselves without telling anyone about it. The reward is knowing that we are pleasing God. Giving of yourself to gain accolades is nothing but self-serving, which is in direct opposition to the principle of giving. Even if others do not see through the facade, God does. Jesus tells his followers this, "Be careful not to do your 'acts of righteousness' before men, to be seen by them. If you do, you will have no reward from your Father in heaven" (Matthew 6: 1).

I think one of the biggest things that touched my heart at my sister Jeanne's funeral was seeing all of the lives that she evidently touched in her work as a teacher. Classes at the school where Jeanne taught were canceled the day of her funeral since so many teachers and students wished to attend her funeral mass. Both her students and colleagues were so moved at her passing and expressed tremendous words of praise for the impact that she and her work had on their lives. My brother Vinnie was very active in his local church. Several weeks after he died, the church held a memorial service to honor him. Just as with my sister, it moved me inside. I was amazed to see all the trouble the church went through to memorialize my brother. I was also deeply touched by the beautiful commentaries that were made about Vinnie's life and to learn of his impact on the lives of his church friends.

Truthfully, it was not until their passing that I realized the effects that my brother's and sister's lives had, and still have, on my life. Only with reflection and living on after them am I coming to understand the impact the twins have had on me. I am sure I have not fully realized it yet. And, by the world's standards, Jeanne and Vinnie were ordinary people. We are not ordinary to God though. He can take the ordinary and, out of it, make something extraordinary if we let Him. We can touch people beyond our reach. We just have to realize that we get only one chance at this life. This is not a dress rehearsal, it's the real thing. We need to make our lives count… now!

Choosing what to do with your life is therefore of critical importance. Many people consider only paths that have the potential to bring them wealth, fame, accolades, or personal pleasure. Nothing is wrong with these things in and of themselves. But when a person's life is motivated totally or even largely by the pursuit of these things, I believe his priorities are out of order. This person is in danger of missing the whole reason of why God put him on this earth. Jesus lived a life of service, not self-indulgence.

When the disciples were arguing among themselves about

who was the greatest, Jesus answered, "If anyone wants to be first, he must be the very last, and the servant of all" (Mark 9: 35). We must seek God for His purposes and plans for our lives. Then we will be fully alive unto Him, with a heart of peace: "When a man's ways are pleasing to the Lord, he makes even his enemies live at peace with him" (Proverbs 16: 7). The Bible also says, "In his heart a man plans his course, but the Lord determines his steps" (Verse 9). It is fine to have dreams and aspirations, but ultimately for our lives to really count for anything worthwhile, we should submit to the will of God for our lives—even when it does not seem to make sense to us. God speaks through His prophet Isaiah, saying, "For my thoughts are not your thoughts, neither are your ways my ways" (Isaiah 55: 8).

What of this notion of our lives being worthwhile? Different people have different standards of what "worthwhile" means. I believe that following God's plan for your life is the most significant thing you can do. You may be a janitor, an architect, a stay-at-home mom, a preacher, an artist, a physician, a business executive, or the President of the United States. Whatever the call on your life, if you are following God's will and doing what you do as unto the Lord, then you are living an invaluable life.

Sometimes people do things that would appear important by the world's standards or in the eyes of people from whom they seek approval. God speaks to this issue through his servant Paul: "If any man builds on this foundation (Jesus Christ) using gold, silver, costly stones, wood, hay or straw, his work will be shown for what it is, because the Day will bring it to light. It will be revealed with fire, and the fire will test the quality of each man's work. If what he has built survives, he will receive his reward" (I Corinthians 3: 12 - 14). The things that we do with our lives and the priorities that we set will be shown forth. Whatever we do that brings glory to God will last; anything less will be burned like stubble and hay.

I will never forget a particular moment in time—it occurred on the morning after my sister Jeanne died. My sister Nancy and I agreed to meet at Jeanne's apartment to pick out a burial outfit for Jeanne. Since I arrived at the apartment first, I had a few moments alone to look around for myself. I walked into Jeanne's bedroom and began to open her closet to see if I could find a nice dress. For some reason, as I looked down at the shoes in her closet, I froze. I could not get my eyes off of her shoes, neatly lined up as if they were waiting for Jeanne to come in any minute and slip them on her feet. I thought back to some of the financial struggles my sister had had in her life and how hard she worked to be able to buy those shoes. In that moment, I also realized that all the hard work that went into getting those shoes didn't really make a hill of beans of difference now. Jeanne could not use them anymore. There she left her shoes, and there they stood. She couldn't use *any* of her stuff anymore. All of her stuff just remained in her apartment—she couldn't take it with her. None of it really mattered in the big scheme of things.

It all seems to matter so much when we are alive though—what we will wear, where we will live, etc.... And while we all have needs and God wants to meet all of our needs, God does not want us to get distracted by worrying about these things. Jesus speaks to this issue when He says, "Therefore I tell you, do not worry about your life, what you will eat or drink; or about your body, what you will wear. Is not life more important than food, and the body more important than clothes" (Matthew 6: 25). Jesus goes on to say that God cares for us and will provide all of these things for us. He ends this section of scripture by saying, "But seek first his kingdom and his righteousness, and all these things will be given to you as well" (Verse 33). The point here is that while we all need to act responsibly for our lives, we also need to trust God. We need to focus on the things of God, and God will take care of us. I pray that all of us, through God's grace, will follow the path that God has carved out for our lives. May we also rightly be remembered as conducting ourselves in a manner worthy and pleasing of Him, putting Him first, above all things.

## Chapter Eight

# My Turning Point

As a school girl, I always enjoyed the subject of math. I liked the idea of taking data from a problem, plugging it into a formula, and producing an answer to that problem. I see the Bible much like math. God has laid down principles in His Word that I see as formulas or road maps for living. When we are faced with trials, we can take the principles God has given us in His Word and apply them in our situation. We will always have victory when we live by His principles.

It took me a while to begin to understand and actually live one principle in particular, but as I have, it has produced much good fruit in my life. The formula or principle goes like this: *The degree to which you submit yourself to God is the degree to which He can work on your behalf and use you for His glory.* The first time I really applied this principle, it produced a spiritual metamorphosis in me. When I applied it towards my grieving process, it produced an emotional metamorphosis. Let us talk about the spiritual transformation or metamorphosis first.

As a young child, my heart was very sensitive to the things of God, and that sensitivity only grew as I grew older. With each passing year, I found myself thirsting to know God in a more intimate way. I knew a lot about Him in my head, but I wanted to experience Him in my heart. I loved and feared God, yet I felt distant from Him. I wanted a deeper relationship with God, but I did not know quite how to obtain it.

---

**The degree to which you submit yourself to God, is the degree to which He can work on your behalf, and use you for His glory.**

---

As a teenager, I became heavily involved in church activities. I actively participated in the C.Y.O. (Catholic Youth Organization) on the local and county levels. I lectured at mass and taught catechism classes to physically, mentally, and emotionally challenged children and teenagers. To my disappointment, my thirst for God was not quenched. I was in church nearly every day, if not for mass, then just to sit in my Father's house to talk with Him. My efforts to reach God and my head knowledge of Him alone could not fill the void inside of me.

At seventeen, I attended a weekend retreat called *Search* with other girls my age, from other local churches. It was there that I *personally* experienced Jesus, I think for the first time in my life. I came to know Him, not only as God the Son, but as a friend and brother, someone who really cared about me. It was an awesome experience. I had always felt that there was more, and suddenly I knew I was right!

As I went through college, I continued to attend church and participate in many of its ministries. I became a Eucharistic minister and now attended these *Search* retreats in a leadership role. I was on many church committees and helped organize many charitable fund raisers. Something was still missing though. While these were good things to be involved in, I felt that my involvement was somehow devoid of real meaning. Yet I didn't know what more I could do. My faith would grow in little spurts, but I was still very hungry for the things of God. I wanted more of what I had experienced on that first *Search* retreat I had attended as a teenager. I wanted a truly satisfying relationship with a *living* God, but I was not sure how to obtain that or if what I wanted was really possible.

Allow me to digress with a brief story that will paint a clear picture of where I was in relationship to God. Coming from Polish and Italian backgrounds, my family followed many wonderful ethnic traditions. One in particular I can remember is after church on Sundays, we would all go to my grandmother's house and have Sunday dinner in her basement. All the aunts, uncles, and cousins were there. You could smell the garlic chicken outside the window, before you even entered the house. When you walked into the kitchen, you could count on the gravy and meatballs simmering on the stove, waiting to be poured over the pasta. After dinner, my grandfather would gather the grandchildren around and tell us stories of when he was a youth back in the "old country." These were wonderful traditions that have left me with some very fond memories.

While some traditions can be good, my religion had also become a tradition for me. Going to church, doing good deeds, praying the prayers I had memorized by rote, and following the rituals that I was indoctrinated in had become as much of a tradition in my life as going to my grandmother's house for Sunday dinner. The difference was, unlike Sunday dinner at Grandma's, the religious traditions left me feeling empty and hollow inside. The very things that I thought I had to do in order to get closer to God actually drew me further away from Him. My overall view of God was still that of a wooden, unapproachable god. That is because the "religious gymnastics" that I thought I had to perform was devoid of the life of God, His Holy Spirit, and the truth of His Word. In a phrase, God had not breathed the breath of His life into our relationship yet. And without the life of the Holy Spirit, I was, in essence, spiritually dead to God.

Let's get back to our timeline. Toward the end of my college career and unbeknownst to my family, I had even considered becoming a nun. (I would have preferred to be a priest, but women are not permitted to be priests.) I figured that total surrender of my earthly desires for marriage and a family of my own would bring me the intimacy I so desired to have with God. I didn't tell anyone then about these thoughts because even now when I tell the story, my friends either politely snicker or laugh out loud. They must know me better than I realize. Anyway, in efforts to explore this possibility, I frequently went away on weekend retreats at convents, with the Sisters of St. Joseph of Chestnuthill.

The last retreat I attended with the sisters was on my 23rd birthday. I was about to graduate from college in just a few months and felt that I needed to make some decisions concerning the direction that my life would go. I had gone away on this retreat with the purpose of deciding once and for all whether or not I would enter religious life or remain a lay person. But I didn't want it to be my decision, I wanted it to be God's. I really needed His guidance.

We had just finished praying together ( I think they called it "vespers") and were dismissed to retire to our rooms for the evening. It was only 9:30 on a Saturday night. I was at the New Jersey shore (one of my favorite places to be), it was my 23rd birthday, and I was sitting in a bare and lonely room in a convent. I was depressed. I didn't know what to do next. I tried praying, but I came up dry. "Lord, where do you want me, and what do you want me to do with my life?" I remember crying out to Him. No answer was forthcoming. Feeling very alone, I opened up the window to get some fresh air. On the street below, a convertible filled with young people passed, playing some very loud Bruce Springsteen music. (He was my favorite musician then.) I wanted to be out there. Yet, I really wanted to know and serve God in a meaningful way. I struggled with thoughts of how to make this desire a reality in my life.

In any case, I just knew that I was in the wrong place. Closing myself off in a convent was not the way for me to draw closer to God. In fact, it just brought me more inner turmoil. The next morning at breakfast, I told the sisters that I would not be returning to the convent; this was not my calling. It was just as well. I was having trouble with the idea of parting with my long hair.

Have you ever felt like you didn't fit in or you didn't know what world you belonged to? I knew I didn't want to live in the secular world, but I didn't feel right about "religious life" either. It was like being in a twilight zone.

Finally, I finished college and began working at my first professional job as a physical therapist. At the same time, I was attending a bible study at the church that I grew up in. All the while, I was still searching to find real meaning in this faith—faith in God—that I claimed to have. "But how could I have faith in a god that I didn't know?" I remember asking myself. It was then that I decided that I *had* to know whether or not God was real. And if God was real, I would have to experience Him in a truly meaningful way. I cried out to God, "God, if you're real, show yourself to me. I want to feel your presence in my heart, and I want to know your purpose for my life."

After that heartfelt prayer to the Lord, He answered me. He sent people across my path and set up circumstances to show me, from the Word of God, how to have a personal relationship with Him. The bible study that I was attending was canceled without warning. Subsequently, a co-worker asked me if I wanted to attend a bible study at his church. I agreed to go, and in no time at all, that was, as they say, the end of that. I began to grow in the things of God like never before. At the bible study, the Word of God was preached and taught. I realized that the *only* way to come to the Father was, not by keeping religious traditions, but through His Son, Jesus Christ. It is the Son that puts us in right relationship with the Father. My spirit was ignited with the fire of God, and my soul was filled with His life! I felt exhilarated, filled with His purpose for my life—I felt alive! I had found peace. I knew that I was Home.

At that time, I became aware of the need to make a commitment to Christ. That is, invite Him into my heart to become my personal Lord and Savior. Though, by the world's standards I had lived a pretty wholesome life, I knew that in God's eyes I was still a sinner and I needed Jesus to cleanse me and change me. While I had known much about Jesus, I had never trusted Him to be Lord and Savior over my life, until making that commitment.

You can know a lot *about* someone without ever having met them. But mere knowledge does not create a personal, intimate relationship with a person. I realized that I had never really "met Him." I had spent over 23 years trying to reach God, attempting to experience Him internally, by "performing" externally. I had it backwards! The Bible says, "'For my thoughts are not your thoughts, neither are your ways my ways,' declares the Lord" (Isaiah 55: 8). It is God who changes us first, internally—He changes our hearts. As a result, we begin to change externally.

I thought that as long as I was a good person, went to church, and tried to help others, I would have fellowship with God and earn heaven. I was trying to obtain heaven by my good works, rather than placing my faith for the salvation of my soul in Jesus Christ *alone*. It was the ultimate deception. When people take illegal drugs or have extramarital affairs or steal, they know they are doing something wrong. That is why they try to hide their actions. But I did not need nor did I want to hide my actions. They were good. The problem was, my "good deeds" and "clean living" blinded me from seeing *my* need for a savior.

The apostle Paul writes about having zeal for God without truth or knowledge in his letter to the Romans: "Brothers, my heart's desire and prayer to God for the Israelites is that they may be saved. For I can testify about them that they are zealous for God, but their zeal is not based on knowledge. Since they did not know the righteousness that comes from God and sought to establish their own, they did not submit to God's righteousness. Christ is the end of the law so that there may be righteousness for everyone who believes" (Romans 10: 1 - 4). I am moved by this passage of scripture because I was like the Israelites that Paul writes about. I had much zeal for God, without truth. Though I had much head knowledge, I had not experienced the knowledge of His truth. I, therefore, sought to establish my own righteousness through my good works.

The difference can be likened to enlisting in the army versus being drafted. I spent years of my own strength trying to enlist myself or hook up with God. Only after I realized that it was the grace of God that calls us to Himself, was I then drafted and engrafted into His family. It is an inside-out experience, not the other way around. Now, any good that I do, I do for the Lord, not for myself. I try to live holy because I love Him and want to serve Him and bring glory to His name. I still go to church and pray, but not because I have to or think it is the right thing to do, but because I *want* to. I have a real and meaningful relationship with my heavenly Father who has loved me with an everlasting love.

Remember the formula: *The degree to which you submit yourself to God is the degree to which He can work on your behalf and use you for His glory.* Once I submitted and gave my heart to the Lord, He fulfilled the longing of my heart and filled the void. Every human being seeks intimacy and oneness with God. However, not every human being knows that this is what they are seeking. I believe that this is why we see so many addictions and compulsions running rampant today. People are trying to fill a void in their lives, and they are using anything that they can get their hands on to fill it. I didn't use drugs, alcohol, sex, material things, or food, like many do, to fill my void. I used "religion." Religion is really man attempting to reach God, when God has already reached down to man, through His Son, Jesus Christ! Once I surrendered my heart to the Lord and allowed Him to "take up residence" there, He was able to work on my behalf and use me for His glory.

Though I wish that, in the blink of an eye, God had made me perfect the day I committed my life to Him, *that is just not how it goes.* I am learning to apply my salvation in stages over the course of my life. As I work out my salvation, read His Word, pray, and fellowship with other believers, my relationship with the Lord grows to heights that I never imagined it could. I still need Jesus to cleanse me and change me every day. Even as a committed Christian, I have been faced with ugly temptations that I have given thought to. I will always need Jesus to overcome.

My spiritual walk is not unlike my walk with grief. As a young girl, though I knew much about God *conceptually*, I had not fully trusted the Lord as my Savior. Likewise, though cognitively I knew God could help me through these terrible losses that I experienced, I was troubled because I had not fully trusted the Lord to do His part in my soul. I was trying to do it myself—to no avail. I had not turned my back on God, nor did I blame Him for what happened to my brother and sister. But neither had I let go enough to allow God to help me. And in the process, I had begun to lose my joy for life. The Bible says, "The joy of the Lord is my strength" (Nehemiah 8: 10 ). Once you lose your joy, you lose your strength. My faith had been weakened because I had given over my joy. I did not realize it then, but it was a test of my faith—whether or not I would trust God to see me through this crisis.

**My faith had been weakened because I had given over my joy.**

Our faith is very much like seed that a farmer plants. Mark 4: 14 - 20 says, "The farmer sows the word. Some people are like seed along the path, where the word is sown. As soon as they hear it, Satan comes and takes away the word that was sown in them. Others, like seed sown on rocky places, hear the word and at once receive it with joy. But since they have no root, they last only a short time. When trouble or persecution comes because of the word, they quickly fall away. Still others, like seed sown among thorns, hear the word; but the worries of this life, the deceitfulness of wealth and the desires for other things come in and choke the word, making it unfruitful. Others, like seed sown on good soil, hear the word, accept it, and produce a crop—thirty, sixty or even a hundred times what was sown."

If we want our faith to grow, we need the seed, which is the Word of God, to be planted in us. That is why we need to read the Bible ourselves and attend church where the Word of God is taught and preached. This is how we get the Word inside of us. Our heart is the ground in which seeds are planted. Is our ground fertile or rocky and full of thorns? Are our hearts soft enough to be open to receive what God wants to show us? Next, all seeds need sunlight and water to grow. Likewise, our souls need the light of the Son and the Holy Spirit.

A seed rests in and gets its nourishment from the ground, and after a time, it germinates and becomes a plant. So it is with our lives. We must rest in the Bible, get the proper nourishment from God's Word, and allow the Holy Spirit to transform us into His new creation: "Do not conform any longer to the pattern of this world, but be transformed by the renewing of your mind" (Romans 12: 2). The Bible says, "Consequently, faith comes from hearing the message, and the message is heard through the word of Christ" (Romans 10: 17).

---

## When I totally surrendered my pain to the Lord, He literally transformed me.

---

Remember that grief is a natural, God-given process, designed to help people cope with loss. This process is meant to be dynamic, however, assisting people *through* a period of pain. It is not meant to keep us *in* the pain forever. I had gotten stuck in that pain for a while and had to learn how to move forward from the place where my heart and soul seemed fixed. I had difficulty letting go. I had allowed my family's trials to choke the truth from the Word of God. I had forgotten about the hope and comfort that God extends to all those who mourn. I had not let the light of the Son and the power of the Holy Spirit renew my mind and transform my situation.

However, as I began to apply the promises of my salvation to my situation of intense grief, I experienced much needed change in my soul realm. *When I totally surrendered my pain to the Lord, He literally transformed me.* As I believed God and emersed myself in His Word, it was He who comforted my soul and transformed my very life. That is because peace always comes when we bathe in the Word of God. His Word tells us many times that He will never leave us or forsake us. When I filled my mind with the promises of His Word, He filled my soul with His joy.

It was at this time that I was reminded of the scripture verses where Jesus was comforting Martha after her brother Lazarus had died. Jesus said, "I am the resurrection and the life. He who believes in me will live, even though he dies; and whoever lives and believes in me will never die. Do you believe this?" (John 11: 25, 26). The truth of the matter is, Jesus is the resurrection and the life. And anyone who believes in Him will live and never die. But notice that Jesus asked Martha, "Do you believe this?" Jesus did not ask Martha this question to get her stamp of approval about what He said. He asked because Jesus knew that if Martha did not believe, that promise would be null and void in Martha's life. *The Word of God will have no effect on our lives if we do not appropriate its truths to our lives.* Likewise, I had heard and read these verses many times over, ever since I was a little girl. It was always a significant piece of scripture to me, but now it had taken on an especially personal meaning to me. I knew that this was my time to appropriate this particular truth into my life in a very deliberate way. I began to see these scripture verses as more than nice "spiritual words" that are often read at funerals. I saw them as the very reason for my faith and the substance in which I hope— that is, eternal life with God, after death, for those who believe. As I applied these words of Christ to my situation, I was freed from that oppressive, all-consuming grief.

> **The Word of God will have no effect on our lives if we do not appropriate its truths to our lives.**

When my sister and brother first died, about 95% of my attention was focused on the pain of my loss. I only allowed probably 5% of my thoughts concerning the twins to comfort me with the notion that I would see them again in heaven. But when I began to celebrate Jeanne's and Vinnie's lives, instead of focusing on their deaths, I started to live again. When I remembered that they had been ushered into heaven and that I would see them again someday, my heart began to sing songs once more. The ratio of happy thoughts compared to sad thoughts has radically shifted because I have allowed it to shift. Now my thoughts concerning my brother and sister are largely focused on happy memories and the comfort of knowing that we will be reunited together in heaven. I still miss them and experience occasional periods of sadness over my loss, but my sadness is not an all-encompassing thing. Once I gave myself permission to live, to be fully alive and without guilt, I was set free! Where the Son is, there is no darkness. The clouds have been removed—it is a different Day!

If your heart is broken, God wants to mend it for you. Once

again, picture a child who takes the pieces of his broken toy to his loving father. He extends his little hands, cradling the broken toy pieces, asking, "Daddy, will you fix it?" That is how we need to be. We need to go to our heavenly Father and give Him the pieces of our broken hearts so He can fix them. He already knows what you need, but He wants you to come to Him and ask. God will not violate your will: "Ask and it will be given to you; seek and you will find; knock and the door will be opened to you. For everyone who asks receives; he who seeks finds; and to him who knocks, the door will be opened. Which of you, if his son asks for bread, will give him a stone? Or if he asks for a fish, will give him a snake? If you, then, though you are evil, know how to give good gifts to your children, how much more will your Father in heaven give good gifts to those who ask him" (Matthew 7: 7 - 11). Simply show Him what is in your heart and ask Him to help you through whatever your situation is. As you call upon the name of the Lord, you will experience joy and peace in your life.

# Chapter Nine

# The Essence of
# Our Lives

M y hopes and prayers are that the words in this book thus far have proven to be comforting, inspiring, and uplifting. I believe, however, that the words in this chapter are by far the most important of all. This chapter has to do with the very essence of life. The Bible says, regarding those of us who are in Christ, "You are a chosen people, a royal priesthood, a holy nation, a people belonging to God, that you may declare the praises of Him who called you out of darkness into His wonderful light. Once you were not a people, but now you are the people of God; once you had not received mercy, but now you have received mercy" (1 Peter 2: 9, 10). These verses, along with many others, give me the privilege to write of the Truth about my Savior and Lord, Jesus Christ. I would like to elaborate on what it really means to trust Jesus as personal Savior and Lord. This salvation, which I received years ago, was the foundation of my deliverance from the bondage of grief.

Remember from the chapter "Fully Alive", that every person

has a spirit. Our spirit lives in a body and possesses a soul. Truly, our bodies are merely the vessels that house our spirits and souls: "The Spirit gives life; the flesh counts for nothing" (John 6: 63). This verse shows that there is more to "life" than this physical life that we live. Life is more than just lungs breathing and a heart beating within a body. It is the Spirit that gives life to our bodies. As a person dies, their spirit and soul leaves their body. As the spirit and soul are removed, their body literally seizes up and ceases to have life. This naturally begs the question, "What happens to the soul and spirit of a person, once that person's body dies?" People have pondered this question for thousands of years. For as many religions that there are in this world, there are probably that many different answers to this same question. I am interested in conveying to you the answer that the Holy Bible, the Word of God, gives us.

First, you should know that everyone's soul/spirit will live on eternally. It is not a matter of *if* but rather *where* they will spend eternity. There is *one* thing, and only one thing, that determines what will happen to your soul and spirit after your body dies. That is, whether or not you have confessed Jesus Christ, the Son of God, as your personal Lord and Savior. Simply put, if you have received Jesus into your heart as your Savior and Lord, you will have salvation. Your soul and spirit will be with God forever in heaven. That is what is meant by the term, "Your soul will be saved." The apostle Paul writes of this: "That if you confess with your mouth, 'Jesus is Lord,' and believe in your heart that God raised him from the dead, you will be saved" (Romans 10: 9).

God loves you so very much. He loves all of His creation. He does not always love what we *do*, but He does love *us*. After all, the book of Genesis tells us that God made man in His own image. God made man so that He could fellowship with man, and man could fellowship with God. But man lost that privilege when he fell through his disobedience to God's Word. Sin, through one man, Adam, spread its trespasses and covered the entire world.

While God loves us, He knows that we are all in need of a Savior. God wants to restore the fellowship that He once had with mankind. That is why He sent Jesus, not just as a symbol to wear around your neck or someone to run to when you are in great need, but as a Savior. Man can be reconciled with God through Jesus Christ: "For God so loved the world that he gave his one and only Son, that whoever believes in him shall not perish but have eternal life. For God did not send his Son into the world to condemn the world, but to save the world through him. Whoever believes in him is not condemned, but whoever does not believe stands condemned already because he has not believed in the name of God's one and only Son" (John 3: 16 - 18).

> **Jesus tells us that no one can see the kingdom of God unless he is born again. That means there are *no exceptions*.**

What does one have to do to receive what God offers? This question is answered during a conversation that Jesus had with a Pharisee named Nicodemus, who went to see Jesus at night. Jesus tells Nicodemus, "I tell you the truth, no one can see the kingdom of God unless he is born again." Nicodemus asked, "How can a man be born when he is old? Surely he cannot enter a second time into his mother's womb to be born!" Jesus answered, "I tell you the truth, no one can enter the kingdom of

God unless he is born of water and the Spirit. Flesh gives birth to flesh, but the Spirit gives birth to spirit" (John 3: 3 - 6).

There has been much controversy over the term "born again." Many people shun this term because they perhaps have had a less than favorable experience when encountering someone who claims to be "born again." My friends, forget the negative things that you may have heard or experienced in the past. Focus on what the Word of God says about being "born again." Jesus tells us that no one can see the kingdom of God unless he is born again. That means there are *no exceptions*.

Please understand that Nicodemus was a good man. He was a respected religious leader of that time. He tried to live a holy life by observing God's laws, the best he could. But he could see that Jesus was preaching a different message than what Nicodemus had been indoctrinated in as a Jew. He wanted to better understand who Jesus was and what His message was really about. Allow me to translate what Jesus was trying to say to Nicodemus that night, in today's vernacular. He was saying, "Nicodemus... religion won't do it for you. Trying to follow the Law won't do it for you. You must be born again." Jesus is saying the same thing to us today. "Your denomination, your church, your temple, your mosque won't save you. You must be born again!"

All "born again" means is that your spirit is birthed from above. We were all born into sin and have a sinful nature. Therefore, spiritually speaking, we are dead to God. We must undergo a *spiritual birth* by believing in Jesus Christ as Savior and making Him Lord of our lives. Hence, our spirits are "born again." Our spirits must be alive unto God if we are to see the kingdom of God!

You might be wondering how you become born again or, in other words, saved. The Bible tells us, "This righteousness from

God comes through faith in Jesus Christ to all who believe" (Romans 3: 22). The Bible also says, "Believe in the Lord Jesus, and you will be saved..." (Acts 16: 31). Once we choose to make room in our hearts for a relationship with Jesus Christ and confess Him as our Savior and Lord, we are born again: "For it is with your heart that you believe and are justified, and it is with your mouth that you confess and are saved" (Romans 10: 10). We are now spiritually alive to God. Spiritually speaking, we are no longer the person we used to be: "Therefore, if anyone is in Christ, he is a new creation; the old has gone, the new has come" (2 Corinthians 5: 17). Hence the term "born again."

Once we are in right relationship with Jesus Christ, we become aware of our sinful nature. But thank God, if we do sin, we can run to the foot of the cross and be cleansed by the blood of Jesus. God tells us in His Word, "If we confess our sins, He is faithful and just to forgive us our sins and to cleanse us from all unrighteousness" (I John 1: 9). God looks upon us, not as our sins deserve, but as cleansed through the finished work of Christ, as he died on a cruel cross for our redemption.

---

**My friends, salvation is not a matter of being good and obtaining righteousness through your own works of goodness.**

---

You might be asking yourself the question, "Why do I need salvation? I am a good person and I try to live a good, decent life." You may even go to church or synagogue every week. Perhaps you have been baptized, confirmed, or barmitzvaed. My friends, remember what Jesus told Nicodemus. Salvation is not a matter of being good and obtaining righteousness through your own works of goodness: "For all have sinned and fall short of the glory of God" (Romans 3: 23). The Bible also says, "All of us have become like one who is unclean, and all our righteous acts are like filthy rags..." (Isaiah 64: 6). Simply put, no matter how good of a life you may lead, you need Jesus to save your soul. We are *all* in need of a savior. No sacrament or ceremony can save you. Why? Because any act of goodness that we might do could never be good enough for us to stand righteous and clean before Almighty God. How good is *good enough*, anyway?

This theology may seem foreign or even harsh compared to what is familiar to you. I know it went against my thinking. Keep in mind, though, that it is the Word of God. This teaching of Jesus went against the theology of the Pharisees too, which is why they could not see the truth. Their own doctrines blinded their eyes and prevented them from receiving the truth of God's Word into their hearts. Jesus said, "Woe to you, teachers of the law and Pharisees, you hypocrites! You are like whitewashed tombs, which look beautiful on the outside but on the inside are full of dead men's bones and everything unclean" (Matthew 23: 27). The Pharisees thought of themselves as so righteous because of having performed what they considered to be pious deeds. They were only concerned with external appearances though, while inside, their spirits were dead to God. Don't allow that to happen to you. The Bible says, "...Man looks at the outward appearance, but the Lord looks at the heart" (I Samuel 16: 7). God wants to change your heart.

The truth is, our hearts have turned from God in rebellion of Him, and they are stained crimson. But believing in Jesus as Savior, who was perfect and without sin and who gave Himself as a sacrifice for us, wipes away our sins and allows us to stand clean and righteous before God. But it is not *our* righteousness, it is righteousness through the shed blood of Christ and not of any sacrament: "For it is by grace you have been saved, through faith—and this not from yourselves, it is the gift of God—not by works, so that no one can boast" (Ephesians 2: 8, 9).

Salvation is not just a nice option, among many, that some may choose to obtain redemption for their sins, while others may choose different options to obtain the same end. Instead, the Bible explains, "Enter through the narrow gate. For wide is the gate and broad is the road that leads to destruction, and many enter through it. But small is the gate and narrow the road that leads to life, and only a few find it" (Matthew 7: 13, 14). All of us need salvation, and the only way to obtain it is through faith in Jesus Christ. Jesus said, "I am the way and the truth and the life. No one comes to the Father except through me" (John 14: 6). Jesus said that He is *the* way, not just *a* way. I pray that your eyes of faith will be unveiled by the Holy Spirit and that you will not just *know about* Jesus Christ, as many do, but allow Him to reign in your heart.

## You don't have to clean yourself up for God, before He can love you or save you.

If you are reading this chapter and feel that the things that you have done in your life are too bad for you to receive God's forgiveness, you are wrong. You are never too far gone, and if you are still breathing, it is not too late! Jesus came to change lives and bring forgiveness and healing to sinners: "...Jesus said, 'It is not the healthy who need a doctor but the sick. I have not come to call the righteous, but sinners'" (Mark 2: 17). You don't have to clean yourself up for God before He can love you or save you. In fact, you are incapable of cleaning yourself up. That is what Jesus does *for you* when you call on His name. Jesus came to bring salvation for anyone who will believe in Him. The Bible promises, "And everyone who calls on the name of the Lord will be saved" (Acts 2: 21).

Consider the thief that hung on a cross next to Christ at His crucifixion. First he rebukes the other criminal and says, "Don't you fear God, since you are under the same sentence? We are punished justly, for we are getting what our deeds deserve. But this man has done nothing wrong." Then he said to Jesus, "Jesus, remember me when you come into your kingdom." Jesus answered him, "I tell you the truth, today you will be with me in paradise" (Luke 23: 40 - 43). The criminal recognized who Jesus really was and opened his heart to Jesus. Then as he called on the name of the Lord, without hesitation, Jesus forgave him and promised him paradise. It is that simple—profound, yet simple.

Your sins cannot keep you from the love and mercy of God unless you choose to walk away from His love and mercy. Conversely, your good works, while they may be commendable, will not earn you a spot in heaven.

Jesus clearly shows us that to see the kingdom of God, our hearts have to be truly right with God. We cannot trust in the fact that we may go to church or temple or that we may live a "good, decent" life. We would be no better than the Pharisees of Jesus' time. Jesus said, "For I tell you that unless your righteousness surpasses that of the Pharisees and the teachers of the law, you will certainly not enter the kingdom of heaven" (Matthew 5: 20).

Maybe you are someone who does not participate in any organized religion, for whatever reason. By now, you may be understanding that this chapter is not about getting you to join some formal religion or a particular church. In fact, it is not about religion at all. Remember that religion is really an attempt of man to reach God, which is impossible. This is about revealing to you that God has reached out to man, through His Son, Jesus Christ. This chapter is showing you how to open your heart and have a personal relationship with the only true and *living* God.

Throughout the Bible, we read about a Messiah. We are shown different "faces" of this Messiah, depending on where we read about Him. In the Old Testament, we read of the Messiah prophetically, as a suffering servant. A Savior who would deliver those who believe in Him from their sins: "But he was pierced for our transgressions, he was crushed for our iniquities; the punishment that brought us peace was upon him, and by his wounds we are healed" (Isaiah 53: 5). In the gospels of the New Testament, we read of an infant Jesus, born of a virgin, otherwise called Immanuel—which means "God with us." The Bible says, "But the angel said to them, 'Do not be afraid. I bring you good news of great joy that will be for all the people. Today in the town of David a Savior has been born to you; he is Christ the Lord'" (Luke 2: 10, 11). Further on in the gospels, we see a crucified Jesus, who bled for your sin and mine: "When they came to the place called the Skull, there they crucified him, along with the criminals—one on his right, the other on his left. Jesus said, 'Father, forgive them, for they do not know what they are doing'" (Luke 23: 33, 34).

Finally, in the book of Revelation, we see again prophetically, a risen and glorified Jesus coming back to the earth: "I saw heaven standing open and there before me was a white horse, whose rider is called Faithful and True. With justice he judges and makes war.... On his robe and his thigh he has this name written: KING OF KINGS AND LORD OF LORDS" (Revelation 19:

11, 16). Here we see Jesus, not as a sacrificial lamb and without singing angels, but as Judge. A very different Jesus that was announced by the shepherds 2000 years ago.

All of these images are true depictions of Jesus, as all have been recorded in the Scriptures through the inspiration of the Holy Spirit. What is crucial to see in all of this, though, is a Jesus who loves you and me more than anything else. More than His very own life. A Jesus who set aside His deity and sacrificed His life for ours: "Who, being in very nature God, did not consider equality with God something to be grasped, but made himself nothing, taking the very nature of a servant, being made in human likeness. And being found in appearance as a man, he humbled himself and became obedient to death—even death on a cross" (Philippians 2: 6 - 8).

Maybe you have wondered why Jesus had to suffer such a cruel death—why salvation for mankind had to come at such a high price. I know I have wondered. I have heard people say, "I don't want to serve a god who says that if I don't confess Jesus Christ as my savior, I will suffer punishment and eternal separation from him." What we need to understand is that God is so very holy. He is righteous. The very nature of holiness and righteousness demands that justice be served and wickedness punished. That punishment is death. But God loves us so much that He provided a way of escape for us: "For the wages of sin is death, but the gift of God is eternal life in Christ Jesus our Lord" (Romans 6: 23). He was willing to sacrifice His one and only Son, whom He loved, to take our punishment. I have a son whom I love very much. I would not want to give him up so someone else could live. When I view God's actions from this angle, I begin to have an appreciation of His immense love for you and for me.

This same Jesus continually shows His love for us by praying or interceding for us at all times: "Christ Jesus, who died—more than that, who was raised to life—is at the right hand of God and is also interceding for us" (Romans 8: 34). He intercedes on our behalf—that *all* would come to know the truth of salvation through Him and that *none* would perish. While the book of Revelation shows Jesus as a victorious Messiah, and rightly so, I believe that Jesus also weeps. I believe that He weeps for all those that He bled for, and yet who still choose to reject Him. Jesus is waiting for you at the door of your heart. Won't you let Him in? He has done all He can—it is up to you. Respond to His love today.

Even though I have experienced much sorrow and grief at the loss of my two siblings, I cannot fully express the peace and joy that I have, knowing that some day, I will see them again in glory. My brother Vinnie made a commitment to Christ early on in his adult life. Though he wasn't perfect, he tried to serve God with his life, and any mistakes that he made before or since that commitment were covered by the precious blood of Jesus.

I was not so sure about where my sister Jeanne stood with God. When she was dying, besides experiencing grief over her sickness and suffering, I was terribly concerned about the condition of her soul. Jeanne was a fine person and accomplished much good in her life. But remember that attaining heaven is not just about "living well." It is about commitment to Christ, and I was not sure that she had made that commitment. She kept her thoughts and beliefs about God very much to herself.

About two weeks before she died, I felt strongly impressed in my spirit to minister the Gospel of Jesus Christ to her. I knew how closed off she had been to this sort of thing, but I prayed and went anyway. When I arrived at my parents' house where she was staying, I found her in the recliner chair in her room.

The shades were drawn because the sunlight hurt her eyes. She was wrapped in a blanket and so sick that she could barely open her eyes or speak. When I tried to make conversation, I could see that she was incapable of much interaction since the cancer had depleted her of most of her energy. But I got down on my knees and I simply asked if I could pray for her and if she would say the sinner's prayer with me. She contemplated my request for a few seconds, and in a barely audible voice, she said, "Go ahead." To my joy, Jeanne reached up her hand to mine and we prayed the prayer of salvation together.

After the prayer, nothing miraculous in the natural sense occurred, but I fully believe that spiritually, Jeanne gave her heart to Christ. I believe that her spirit was transformed and made alive unto God. Two weeks later, Jeanne expired. When her body died, I believe her spirit and soul went to be with the Lord.

---

## One cannot rest till the day she or he finds Christ.

---

Thomas Watson said, "That it is best to die, than to lose the purpose of life." All of us must find that purpose while living on this earth. A person is never satisfied till she or he finds rest. The dove that was initially let out of Noah's Ark could not find rest till the day that it returned back to the Ark. It is the same with our souls that were made for eternity. One cannot find rest till the day she or he finds Christ. I have confidence that Jeanne and Vinnie have found their rest. They are with God, and I will see them again. It is *walking* in this knowledge that has restored my peace and joy. It is allowing Jesus to have preeminence, even over this area of my life, that has broken the chains of grief in my life.

Yes, there is pain at the loss of life. But Christians do not have to mourn as the world mourns. We may experience sadness and pain from our losses, and we need to process and express that pain in a healthy way. But we do not have to be overcome by a spirit of grief. The prophet Isaiah writes of Jesus, the coming Messiah, "Surely he took up our infirmities and carried our sorrows" (Isaiah 53: 4). Other translations say, "he has born our griefs." Jesus bore our griefs so that we don't have to. Hallelujah! It is up to us to walk in that truth.

Our mourning *can* turn into joy at the realization that this life is not the end and that we will be together again in heaven. You can have this confidence too, for yourself, by asking Christ into your heart and, for your loved ones, by sharing the love of Christ with them. Don't waste anymore time. Why not make the decision for Jesus right now and experience the love and peace of God in your life, like you never have before? Despite what your earthly life is like, the only thing that will matter in the end is whether or not you walk with the Lord. For truly, this is *the essence of our lives*.

# Chapter Ten

# There Is Hope

One of my purposes for writing this book was to give you a true sense of hope. The theme of hope has been consistently woven throughout the chapters of this book. There is hope that you can experience joy in your life, whatever the circumstances. The love of God brings hope. There is still a chance for you to love today, even if you missed the chance to love yesterday. There is hope for you to live again, even when someone that you may have loved very much has stopped living. You don't have to just exist, but you can be fully alive! You can seize today and make a happy memory for yourself or someone else—an opportunity that you might not have seized yesterday nor get tomorrow. There is a real hope that you can heal, from the inside out. Experiencing significant and even devastating loss does not preclude you from healing. Healing is for the hurting, not for the whole. *The deeper the hurt, the greater the healing that is available to you!*

There is a hope that we can make our lives count for something good in this life. Whatever our past, there is a hope for both our present and our future. Amidst the brokenness and pain of this world, we have hope that God will meet our needs and heal our pain, right here in this life. We also have a future hope that we will spend eternity with God in heaven if we have put our trust in Jesus Christ alone as our Lord and Savior. Then every tear will be wiped away, forever!

> **Experiencing significant and even devastating loss does not preclude you from  healing.**

We become born again by opening our hearts to Christ. It is then that we cross over from death to life: "I tell you the truth, whoever hears my word and believes him who sent me has eternal life and will not be condemned; he has crossed over from death to life" (John 5: 24). This first grain of truth comes into our hearts through the Holy Spirit. In order for this truth to grow, we need to listen to God's Word. When we first come to know the Lord, we are like babes in God and sometimes the Bible can seem difficult to understand. But as a baby listens to his parents when they talk, after a few years the child grows and understands his parents and learns how to talk as well. It is the same with those who come to the Lord. We have to read the Bible over and over again and the Bible begins to talk to us. (God talks to us through His book.)

Becoming a good speaker requires that we become a good listener first. It is the same with the Bible. If we want communion with God, we must listen first. Then we have communion with our heavenly Father just like we would with a natural father. As we keep feeding on God's Word, we grow in His knowledge and grace. We grow strong because we know whom we have trusted now. Then our re-birth is matured. It makes us feel good but *not* proud.

It is a wonderful feeling to have tasted the grace of God. You might remember as church lets out, the priest always says, "The grace of God be with you." That is the grace we must receive in order to be secured.

Since losing my sister Jeanne and brother Vinnie, I am a different person. I believe that my life has been forever changed. This is not all bad because through the struggles and losses, I have learned to trust Him in ways that I never have before. I must repeat what I wrote in the preface of this book. That is, I do not claim to have fully mastered the lessons written down in this book or to live a perfect Christian life. However, as I press on towards the goal of life in Christ, through His grace, I trust that He will make me more like Himself.

Though I have been damaged, I am not defeated. Though I have been knocked down, I am not knocked out. As I trust and let God heal my heart as it needs, I experience a higher and more profound level of His strength and glory in my life.

A final word to those of you who are experiencing pain in your life: I cannot take the pain from you, though I wish that I could. But there is a greater One who can. You will have to walk through it, just as I did, but He can help you find your way. Jesus is available to walk with you and even carry you as you need. We are instructed by the apostle Paul, "Be strong in the Lord and in His mighty power" (Ephesians 6: 10). The power of the love of God is stronger than any force that I know—it has the power to set us free: "And now I commend you to God and to the word of His grace, which is able to build you up and to give you the inheritance among all those who are sanctified" (Acts 20: 32).

If we let God be God in our lives, our state of grief can be transformed into His condition of glory. Indeed, *you too* can go *from grief to glory*!

# Prayer of Salvation

**Lord Jesus, I am a sinner. I believe that you died for my sins. I repent and ask you to forgive all of my sins. I trust you now, as Savior and Lord of my life. Come into my heart and change me into the person you want me to be.**

If you prayed the prayer above with a sincere heart, you are now born again. You are at the beginning of a whole new life in Christ. To deepen this relationship you should:

• Read the Bible everyday.

• Talk to God in prayer everyday.

• Attend church where Jesus Christ, Lord and Savior is preached, and where you can worship with other believers in spirit and in truth.

• Tell others about Christ and allow His love to show through you.

God Bless You!

If you would like to send your comments to the author or for information about having Francine Bouwense minister at your church, seminar or support group, you may write her at:

Francine Bouwense
P.O. Box 82
Chester, New Jersey  07930-0082

Printed in the United States
780600001B